Wings of the Spirit

Wings of the Spirit

DEVOTIONS
FOR PERSONAL
AND GROUP USE

✓ ✓ ✓

Wallace Fridy

ABINGDON PRESS — NEW YORK • NASHVILLE

WINGS OF THE SPIRIT

Copyright © 1963 by Abingdon Press

Library of Congress Catalog Card Number: 63-16375

SET UP, PRINTED, AND BOUND BY THE
PARTHENON PRESS, AT NASHVILLE,
TENNESSEE, UNITED STATES OF AMERICA

to ♥♥♥

Mrs. Thomas Cannon Baskette
(*née* ILA HOPE PUGH)
my wife's mother

✓✓✓

PREFACE

There is so much in life that adds weight to our spirits, that takes from life a sense of freshness, that brings a measure of boredom robbing men of an awareness of God. It is hoped that this book will help to give wings to the spirit.

It is hoped that these pages will assist those who read them to discover the power and presence of God, which gives wings to the spirit. It is sent out believing that the joy of living is determined not so much by what life brings to us, but by the attitude we bring to life; not so much by what happens to us, but by the way we look at what has happened. Actually, what life does to us depends in large measure on what life finds in us, and what life finds in us is dependent on our outlooks, our attitudes, our motives.

It is hoped that what is written here will deepen the faith of those who read it in the Good News of the Gospel, as James S. Stewart puts it, "that God has invaded history with power; that in the Cross the supreme triumph of naked evil has been turned once and for all to irrevocable defeat; that Christ is alive now and present through His spirit; that through the risen Christ there has been let loose into the world a force which can transform life beyond recognition."

These chapters have been prepared for personal use, as well as resource material for those responsible for leading worship services. It is hoped, too, that busy pastors may find here suggestions in sermon preparation. At the close of each chapter are worship aids to assist the leader in conducting worship services, and the prayers included may also be helpful in private devotions.

These messages have all arisen out of human need, from the experiences of a pastor with his people. They have been shared in amplified form from the pulpit, and in their present form with a much wider audience through the columns of the daily press. They are sent out with the prayer that those who read them in private or who are led by them in group worship may discover help in finding the meaning of life and the strength to face it victoriously.

WALLACE FRIDY

7 7 7

CONTENTS

9

I

Looking straight beyond

The real meaning of life depends upon the outlook we have on it. It is a matter of proper focus. This focus in life has to do with three areas of experience—the past, the present, and the future. There is a statue in a certain town, the base of which is a triangular stone, and on the three sides are inscribed these words: "To the past, Mindful; to the present, Faithful; and to the future, Hopeful." Here we have the proper relationship expressed.

"To the past, Mindful." If we would live well in the present we cannot ignore the past. Being mindful of it helps guide our way in the present. Without memory of the past our lives would be empty and bleak. Without memory we forget our heritage; we forget all that we learn. To lose sight of the past the businessman would fail, love would grow cold, and life would be barren.

"To the present, Faithful." To be faithful to the present is to do the best you can with what you have. It is to follow the light you now have, to do the duty nearest you as you see it. It is "to serve the present age, our calling to fulfill." All that God ex-

11

pects of us is to be faithful to the truth as we understand it, to give the best that we have to the highest that we know.

"To the future, Hopeful." Hope is a necessity in life. We cannot live well and be faithful to the present unless we have hope for the future. When you take hope away, you destroy a chance for a future.

We cannot possibly separate ourselves from the past, the future, or the present. The life we live today is related to that of yesterday and determines that of tomorrow. But our main theme today has to do with looking straight beyond. It centers on the third inscription at the base of the statue: "To the future, Hopeful."

In the first place, all of us know hope as a friend. It is our hope of new health that keeps us going when a loved one is sick. It is hope of return that holds us steady when we send our loved ones to far-off places. It is hope for a job when unemployed that helps men keep their sanity. It is hope for better days that sustains us when we are caught in low moods. It is hope of immortality that comforts us in sorrow. Indeed, as Bishop Watson has said, "Hope is like the cork to the net, which keeps the soul from sinking in despair. . . ."

In the second place, the Christian faith is one of hope. Paul says that "we are saved by hope." He looked at life first with a view of realism and even skepticism. He had to be shown. Yet, he wrote in his letter to the Romans, "We are saved by hope."

This pull of hope comes from God. He believes that there is nothing too good to believe about God, that God can be depended upon, that the "Creator who keeps faith in the appetites of the body and the instincts of the birds will not play false with the deepest desires of the soul." The Christian faith is one of hope that tells us that no matter how complex the problem, with God there is always a way out. It tells us that God always has the last word in life.

Paul writes, "Tribulation worketh patience; and patience, experience; and experience, hope." (Rom. 5:3, 4) It took tribulation to teach Paul patience Some time ago there was a lady in a hospital who had never been there before. This was her first experience. It was almost more than she could stand. She was impatient. But there were others in that same hospital who through the tribulation of illness had become patient. It is often through forced retirement or forced quietness that the soul discovers the hidden depths of the spirit which otherwise might have remained uncovered. Some are discovering through illness what John Milton discovered in his day through blindness, that "they also serve who only stand and wait." Yes, we can learn that tribulation bringing forced delays can add richness and harmony to life through patience.

"Tribulation worketh patience; and patience, experience." James Moffatt translates it like this: "Endurance produces character." Character does not come with the mere passing of time. It has to be achieved. Patience plays its part.

Then comes Paul's third step, "experience, Hope." It is the testimony of the ages that when character has been achieved, there has been patience; and when patience has ripened into character, then hope followed.

Here is the sufferer who through months and years of illness has grown patient and kind, and who does not doubt the goodness of God. Here is a woman who lost her sight. She had never seen her two sons, except as she traced their features with her sensitive hands. What a wonderful mother she was. One day she was heard singing in a little country church. Lifting up her untrained voice here are the words she was singing: "Hope on; let us not repine; the morn will come, and the sun will shine." How could a blind woman sing like that? God placed hope within her heart.

"Now abideth hope." This is that which makes us know that God is good, and that he can take these lives of ours and link them to something greater than we are.

AIDS TO WORSHIP

HYMNS: "Saviour, Like a Shepherd Lead Us"
         "He Leadeth Me"
SCRIPTURE: Rom. 5:1-5

14

A PRAYER

Eternal God, in whom we live and move and have our being, thou hast been our dwelling place in all generations, before the mountains were brought forth or thou hadst formed the earth and the world, even from everlasting to everlasting, thou art God.

We come before thee this day unworthy of thy love; we come stained by temptations which so easily beset us; we come feeling need of thee—thy power, thy strength, and thy forgiveness. Thou knowest us better than we know ourselves. Thou knowest our needs and art standing ready to help us.

Take us this day and lift us upward. Do thou:

> Strengthen our steps,
> Enlarge our visions,
> Quicken our hopes,
> Purify our motives.

Remind us of the things which do not change, and secure us to life's unfading treasures. In the name and in the spirit of Christ we pray. AMEN.

2

Two kinds of power

Henry Sloan Coffin reminds us that there are two kinds of spiritual energy which correspond to two forms of physical energy—dynamic and static. One is the force to do, and the other the force to endure.

He tells us that for years his study window on Morningside Heights in New York City looked up the Hudson River to George Washington Bridge. Here he saw the two varieties of energy. There was the steady stream of traffic going back and forth over that bridge from Manhattan Island to New Jersey. There were buses, cars, and trucks disclosing power for the business of mankind. Here was the force to do—an energy so needed in our world today.

Then there was the bridge—a vast structure of steel upheld by miles and miles of wire no bigger than a man's little finger—enough to girdle the globe more than four times—on which the heavy traffic traveled back and forth. This bridge with its tons of concrete, its jarring traffic, and even the fierce winds that swept against it, was able to stand. Further, it was so built to undergo the changes in temperature contracting the steel from midnight to noon. From the heat of midsummer up to 120 degrees Fahrenheit to 15 degrees below zero in midwinter this bridge was designed to be strong and to stand.

Here we have two types of power—power to achieve and power to sustain. Christians must possess these two kinds of spiritual energy. They must forever be about the Father's business going wherever and doing whatever his Holy Spirit leads them to. Then they must bear the weight that comes to them, the pressures of life that beat upon them, and the changes in climate to which they are exposed every day of their lives. They need power to do and power to endure.

And the bridge with its traffic represents the kinds of power needed and illustrated in scripture in the eleventh chapter of Hebrews. In the thirty-third and thirty-fourth verses we have these words: "Who through faith subdued kingdoms, wrought righteousness, obtained promises . . . turned to flight the armies of the aliens." Dynamic energy we see here.

Then in the thirty-fifth and thirty-sixth verses we have these words: "Others were tortured, not accepting deliverance; and others had trial of cruel mockings and scourgings, yea, moreover of bonds and imprisonment." This is the static energy needed then and needed today by present-day Christians who are compelled to take it and to take it again.

Let us look more closely at these two types of

17

power. *In the first place, here is the power needed to achieve or to do.* When Jesus gave us our marching orders to go into all the world to witness for him, he also promised the power needed. In the eighteenth verse of the last chapter of Matthew we read: "And Jesus came and spake unto them, saying, All power is given unto me in heaven and in earth," then there follows, "Go ye therefore." And in the twentieth verse it reads: "Lo, I am with you alway, even unto the end of the world."

There is work to be done for God in helping him build his kingdom here on earth. There is evil that needs to be revealed and fought. There are people who are hurt by life and the forces of life, many of them evil forces, who need help. There are churches to be built and missions to be established. God's work needs the consecrated energy of countless millions of people to carry it on. This is the power to achieve so needed in our time. It is terribly easy to be weary in well doing, and we need the power to do for God what he wants us to do, the power to be about the Father's business.

In the second place, power is needed to sustain, or to endure. Again in Hebrews we read: "Others were tortured, not accepting deliverance; and others had trial of cruel mockings and scourgings, yea, moreover of bonds and imprisonment." This is the static energy needed not only by those early Christians but by us today. We are called on to take it and to take it again and again.

18

This power to endure is not just one that would save men from danger or rather give them the strength to stand in the face of it, but it is also a power needed to sustain men in the face of temptation. We live under the constant pressure to conform, to go along with the group, to accept ideas of the majority whether it agrees with what we may know to be right or not.

Jesus faced his temptations in the wilderness. Following Jesus those early Christians faced with similar temptations would not compromise and walk with the crowd, even in the face of persecution. Listen to these words of Paul's in a letter to the Roman Christians: "And be not conformed to this world: but be ye transformed by the renewing of your mind, that ye may prove what is . . . [the] will of God." In Phillips' translation we have it put like this: "Don't let the world around you squeeze you into its own mold, but let God remold your minds from within."

Then, too, we need that static energy or that power to sustain us when we face suffering and trouble. Surely it is our faith that God can either heal our wounds and restore our health or give us the strength to withstand them. What would we do without his power and his presence to see us through —this power to endure!

This power comes to us through faith in Christ. Paul put it like this, "I can do all things through Christ who strengtheneth me." Moffatt translates it like this: "In Him who strengthens me, I am able for anything."

AIDS TO WORSHIP

HYMNS: "All Hail the Power of Jesus' Name"
          "Faith of Our Fathers"
SCRIPTURE: Heb. 11:1-6; 33-36

A PRAYER

Eternal God, thou who art the light of the minds that know thee, the strength of the wills that serve thee, and the life of the souls that love thee, help us so to know thee that we may truly love thee, and so to love thee that we may fully serve thee, whom to serve is perfect freedom.

Grant that we may fashion our lives according to thy will and purpose. O God, we are wearied with the demands made upon us, the tasks our hands have had to do, the temptations which confront us, the decisions which claim our attention, the rush and hurry of daily life—all these have taken heavy toll upon our spirits.

We pray that this would be an hour of renewal, that we may find here water from an everflowing spring that would quench our thirst, food from thy boundless storehouse that would nourish our spirits, and light from thy limitless wisdom that would illumine our pathway. In the name and in the spirit of Christ we pray. AMEN.

3
Cups of cold water

In the forty-second verse of the tenth chapter of Matthew we have these words: "And whosoever shall give to drink unto one of these little ones a cup of cold water only in the name of a disciple, verily I say unto you, he shall in no wise lose his reward."

Here Jesus is stressing the divine evaluation of the elementary kindly service. Now anyone who has been in the hot season of the year to the Holy Land can see with deeper insight what Jesus was talking about in "a cup of cold water." In this dry and thirsty land this act of kindness has great meaning.

I recall traveling with a group one day from Amman, in Jordan, to Petra some 180 miles south with only a bottle of hot water to quench our thirst. Having been delayed for four hours because of road repairs, the whole trip took us from seven o'clock in the morning until twelve midnight, and all the water available was a little warm water from a bottle. Indeed, we knew what Jesus meant by this figure of speech—"A cup of cold water."

But here he was using it as a symbol, and this symbol was for *kindness*. It is meeting life at a point of need. Kindness makes our Christian witness convincing. Archbishop William Temple has claimed that Christianity is the most "materialistic" of all faiths. He means, of course, that it finds the largest place for matter. It recognizes the place of the physical in life. Christianity cannot, like some religions, be undisturbed in the presence of physical need. Halford Luccock once wrote that the cup of cold water must go with the bread of life.

To be sure life at times may seem a barren and parched affair with no cups of water. Sometime ago a man came into a minister's study and poured out his burden of woe. He had been on top and now was on the bottom. Life really held no meaning. Sometimes he wondered if he should take his own life.

He admitted that what was happening to him was due to his own sins. Payday was at hand. He said that years before when he was in a thriving business, he would not hesitate to cheat a man if it was to his advantage to do so. "Oh, I'm paying for my sins. That I know," he reflected.

Then he said, "This is a cruel world. Get down and nobody helps you up."

Now, of course, when we look at the misery and heartache in our world today, when we see the conflict that rages between nations, both in a cold and hot way, we agree with this visitor that this is a cruel world. College and high school graduates are often warned about the cruel world in which they are entering. And sometimes in jest they say, "I'm going out into this cruel world."

But having said that, let us not forget that there is kindness too. Where there are forces which would destroy, there are also forces that would heal. Where there are ruthless men, there are also charitable men. Though there are those who push men down, there are also those who lift men up.

Along the journey of life we see this cup of cold water given in unexpected places. I saw this happen in the Middle East, that part of the world which is predominantly Moslem in religion.

We had been riding some four or five hours over a dusty and dry highway. Over our mouths were damp handkerchiefs, and, in fact, most of the time we had to breathe through a handkerchief. We had little water in the car, and what we had was in bottles.

As we rounded a curve we saw a man who was tending sheep running toward the highway. Our driver stopped, for he understood the signal of this bedouin shepherd. As he got out of the car, he took a bottle of water with him and gave this man a drink. Indeed, it was a cup of cold water given in a foreign land.

In the tenth verse of the twelfth chapter of Romans Paul writes "Be kindly affectioned one to another with brotherly love; in honour preferring one

23

another." Here Paul is giving emphasis to the fact that there is no greater need in the world today than kindness and thoughtfulness extended one to another. To be sure the world starves in some quarters for food, for economic aid, for material welfare, but greater than these needs is that of love and kindness. A kind word, a thoughtful deed, a genuine appreciation, a friendly handclasp, a token of encouragement—such lifts in unexpected places and from unexpected sources have often changed the course of many men's lives.

George Matthew Adams, the columnist, has said that the kindness shown him at a critical time by a stranger whom he knew only by reputation was the means of his finishing his college course.

Kindness is really a positive thing. It costs so little to mean much. We must think about it and cultivate it. Let's try to go out of our way to be kind to others. Let us say with William Penn, "I expect to pass through this life but once. If therefore, there be any kindness I can show, or any good thing I can do to any fellow being, let me do it now, and not defer or neglect it, as I shall not pass this way again."

AIDS TO WORSHIP

HYMNS: "Dear Lord and Father of Mankind"
             "Saviour, More than Life to Me"
SCRIPTURE: Matt. 10:39-42

A PRAYER

Almighty God, who hast given us this good land for our heritage, who hast provided for us all the good things of life, forgive us for our failure to share with all men what thou doth provide.

We have made use of the resources of thy earth, have tilled the soil, hewn the forest, and produced in plenty the necessities of this life. The mind of man has mastered the machine and with it filled his barns and storehouses to overflowing. Yet, our Father, some of thy children are crying today for bread which has been stored, fruit which has decayed, and meat which has spoiled.

For all these things forgive us. We have made use of thy bounty in production but have defied thy laws in distribution. Grant us wisdom and the will needed to make adjustment. Give us concern, O Lord, for all thy children, who are our brothers. In the spirit of Christ, we pray. AMEN.

4
God—our refuge and strength

A little girl was describing to her friend the location of the church she was attending. She said, "It is the church down the street that has a plus mark on top."

What a wonderful way to describe a church, for surely the cross represents a plus mark in life. And what a marvelous way to describe a Christian as being a person who has a plus quality about him.

Jesus was thinking of this difference when in the sermon on the mount he said, "For if ye love them which love you, what reward have ye? do not even the publicans the same? And if ye salute your brethren only, what do ye more than others? do not even the publicans so?"

This phrase "what do ye more than others" suggests to us that there should be something different about the Christian. There should be a certain radiance about his life that sets him off from those who do not profess to be.

Let us explore briefly how God does become our refuge and strength and Christ makes a difference.

In the first place he makes a difference, for in him we find a strength that helps us stand the loads of life.

It is our faith that beyond our fondest imaginations and expectations, when the unwanted comes upon us, ready for our use are resources from the hand of God that will enable us to see it through. God does not grant to us any experience in life, but he offers resources to help us see it through.

Not long ago a person faced with the tragic death of her husband and child and with a future that seemed to many so very hopeless, said "You know, if someone had told me before this happened that I could have stood it, I would not have believed it." This good woman was discovering what it meant to place herself in the hands of God, to believe what he says when he promised, "Come unto me, all ye that labour and are heavy laden, and I will give you rest."

Although God doesn't save us from trouble we do know that he saves us in trouble. In him is strength that helps us stand the loads of life.

Again we find in Christ the strength that helps us withstand the temptations of life. He gives us not only the insight and a sensitive conscience to see our duty, but he also offers us the power to see it through.

In Lloyd Douglas' *The Robe*, Justus, talking to Marcellus, says, "I only know that he is alive. . . . Sometimes I feel aware of him, as if he were close by. . . . It keeps you honest. . . . You have no temptation to cheat anyone, or lie to anyone, or hurt anyone

27

—when, for all you know, Jesus is standing beside you." Marcellus says that such would make him very uncomfortable. Then Justus replies: "Not if that presence helped you defend yourself against yourself. It is a great satisfaction having someone standing by to keep you at your best."

In the second place, through Christ we gain a respect that restores our faith in men.

Certainly if anyone should have been discouraged by the failures and faults of men, it would have been Jesus. Though he was betrayed, denied, and crucified, yet, there was such a love and respect for men that he said hanging upon the cross, "Father, forgive them; for they know not what they do."

Contrast his view of man with those who discount the value of human beings. There are cynics who say that we are merely sick flies on a dizzy wheel. Materialists would have us believe that we are only a bundle of electrons with no soul. Some would-be psychologists, certainly no Christian ones, say that man is a jumble of stimuli-response-reactions with no enduring value.

But over against such disparagement of human nature, we come face to face with the Christian conception of man. No other interpretation is so satisfying. Who are we? We are children of God. We are creatures of infinite worth because we are important to God.

Jesus sought through comparison to give us some idea of God's love for us. "If ye . . . know how to give good gifts unto your children, how much more shall your Father which is in heaven. . . ." Yes, if parents will sacrifice for their children, how much more God! If a man will lay down his life for his friend, how much more God!

Lacordaire once dramatized this truth of God's love when he said, "If you would wish to know how the Almighty feels towards us, listen to the beating of your own heart and add to it infinity."

So, in Christ, we find a respect that restores our faith in men.

And finally, *through Christ we gain a confidence that calms our fears.* Here was the Master on board the vessel when a fierce storm arose and the disciples were afraid. Then, you remember, Jesus came on deck and said, not only to the heaving waves but to the distressed disciples, "Peace be still." He calmed their fears.

This confidence comes to us today from the realization that we worship a living Lord and not a dead one. Martin Niemoller once said that what we need more than anything else is the experience that "Christ is the living Lord, not just for today but for all time."

Leslie Weatherhead puts it like this in his book *When the Lamp Flickers:* "He does not wave to us from the past; he beckons us from the future." He is alive, here and now, moving and working among men. Confidence then comes to us when we know

29

that we labor and live and love and laugh not alone—that he is always standing by.

So today, mid the strain and stress of our daily living, we find our Lord, if we but let him, calming our fears and making us know that "God is our refuge and strength, a very present help in trouble." This is the difference that Christ makes.

AIDS TO WORSHIP

HYMNS: "Come, We That Love the Lord"
          "Blest Be the Tie That Binds"
SCRIPTURE: Matt. 5:43-48

A PRAYER

Eternal God, into thy holy presence we come lifting our common supplications unto thee. Thou knowest the needs of our hearts, our fears, our anxieties, our unanswered perplexities. The burdens we carry are known by thee. The heartaches which disturb us are not foreign to thy knowledge.

Many of us, our Father, are heavy laden with problems too great to bear. Some of us face illness. And some of us are confronted with decisions in which thy guidance is sorely needed. We know not where to turn but to thee, remembering thy invitation—"Come unto me, all ye that labour and are heavy laden, and I will give you rest." Speak to our needs this day as we seek to open our hearts unto thee. In Christ's name, we pray. AMEN.

5
Life has another factor

There is an idea all to prevalent to-day that a person cannot rise higher than his heredity and his environment—that he cannot break through the social status of the home or community in which he lives. There are many young people defeated in life before they start by thinking that life has en-closed them within the confines of the culture or status of their family, community, or economic level.

Now to be sure we are largely the products of our environment and heredity. The surrounding condi-tions under which a person lives contribute more to the making of personality than most people are will-ing to admit. Climate, for example, stimulates or depresses personality.

Our social environment also determines to a great extent personality. This is a combination of factors such as language, literature, religion, occupational opportunity, moral standards, habits of thought and action. The fact is, we develop in such a social context.

Then we have to reckon with heredity. Each of us has certain characteristics which were passed on to us—such as color of the skin, color of the eyes, the texture of the hair, the shape of the head, the general size of the body. Size itself produces effects. The presence of a large man tends to overawe a small man.

And, the native endowment of intelligence cannot be ignored. It is an inborn capacity. We inherit it. The quality of intelligence remains constant throughout life. Knowledge is acquired, but intelligence is a general ability to effectively apply this knowledge. Thus, this potential degree of intelligence is native and unalterable.

Yet, having said this about environment and heredity, it does mean that we cannot rise above them. And most of the time when we are thrown in this mood of despair and frustration, we are leaving out God and thinking in terms of only heredity and environment. What we really do is to rule out God. We count merely on human resources and physical supplies and fail to count God in. Now it is this third factor, God, which gives to life unity, purpose, meaning, and power.

Let us turn to an outstanding example of one who found this to be true. His name was Paul. This third factor as he found it in Christ, gave to Paul's life meaning, purpose, and power. It enabled him to transcend his past and to overcome his present. His secret was given expression in his words found in Gal. 2:20: "It is no longer I who live, but Christ who lives in me." This became the controlling factor of his life.

Persecution, loneliness, banishment, misunderstanding, and deprivation—are all hard to endure, but they could not shatter his personality nor overcome him with despair. He was thrown into prison more than once; five times he was given forty stripes at the hands of one of the Jews. He was beaten with rods; he was shipwrecked three times; he suffered from hunger and cold. He withstood the false accusations of his converts. He suffered the treachery of false brethren. But none of these nor any combination could separate him from God.

Here we have a man who to be sure was largely the product of his environment and heredity, but through Christ was able to rise above them. This third element is God and man's response to him. This is one of man's chief glories, and that is, he can respond to life and not merely react.

There is no way to explain Dwight L. Moody except through the power of his third factor. He was an ordinary shoe salesman. No one knowing him in his earlier years would have guessed that this simple little man would later become an evangelist whose influence would reach around the world. In every land today there are men and women whose lives were transformed because of the direct or indirect influence of Dwight L. Moody. It was William T. Grenfell, a self-centered London physician, who was transformed through the influence of Moody and who became a devoted doctor for Christ's sake in Labrador. What made the difference in Moody's life? It was God, who through Christ changed him into a flaming evangelist. His life can be explained in no other way.

Maybe some of you feel that life for you is futile. You are in despair. Your past and your inheritance are not what you would have liked them to be. You no longer gain joy out of living. You are ready to throw in the towel. Well, here is hope for you. Don't rule God out. For he can take what seems to be a hopeless, helpless broken man and make him whole again. He can take a person whose heritage pulls him down and whose surroundings are not conducive to good living and make him over again.

AIDS TO WORSHIP

HYMNS: "Jesus Calls Us"
           "O Jesus, I Have Promised"
SCRIPTURE: Phil. 3:13-17

A PRAYER

Eternal God, in whom there is no darkness, and from whom we find light for life's journey, thou art great in power, unlimited in wisdom, and infinite in all the resources of thy being.

Through countless channels thou dost seek our lives, at many a door thou dost stand and knock. Help us to know that life's most important quest is finding thee and being found by thee. With gratitude we turn our thoughts toward thy mercy and love made known in so many ways. We know that thou art with us and blessing us even when we are unaware of thy presence. We are confident that thou dost will for our lives all that is good. We are assured through Christ our Lord that thou dost go with us in all life's experiences.

Help us to see with clearer eyes and keener visions that thou art the Way, the Truth, and the Life. Give to us the renewed conviction that life will work only as thou hast planned it, and as Christ hast made it known unto us. In his name, we pray. AMEN.

6
We are citizens of heaven

The story of England's colonization of this country is a romantic and thrilling one. For those who left the shores of home and hearth for an unknown land they had the promise of adventure, and adventure they found. It was no armchair affair, it was no "white collar job"; it was not for weaklings, for only stout hearts survived.

So it is with the Christian faith. It is high adventure, and one reason for this is found in Paul's letter to the Philippians, where he writes, "But we are a colony of heaven" (Moffatt). He is saying that our real citizenship is in heaven. He reminds the Philippians that although they live on earth, their real home is elsewhere.

To these Romans, though miles away from Rome in Macedonia, his words have special meaning, for they prided themselves on being Roman citizens. Of course Paul is conscious of the abiding ties of city and state upon them and recognizes the claims of the earthly state; nevertheless, he says that as Christians our major claim comes from a higher kingdom.

Our task then as colonizers is to try to bring God's kingdom to earth. Ours is to take the world for Christ, to unfurl his flag so that the kingdoms of this world will become the kingdom of our Lord and his Christ.

Let us then look more closely into the words of our text: "But we are a colony of heaven." What does it mean to be here on earth good citizens of heaven?

In the first place, to be true to our real kingdom we must be true to the King of that kingdom. Beyond the claims of earthly rulers comes the claims of God upon us. To him we owe our first loyalty and allegiance. From him we gained the chance to live. From him we were loaned life which he expects us to return to him. His claims upon us far outweigh the claims of man or state. They are supreme.

To be sure, the King has given us the freedom to reject his claim, to refuse to acknowledge him as Lord and Ruler. We can set ourselves up as our own rulers. We can deify man. But though we refuse God's claim upon us, we cannot escape it. For when we refuse it, we are destroyed by our own sin and wrongdoing. Indeed, "We are restless until we rest in him." And when a man sets himself up as the center of his world, then he starts on a journey that leads to a dead-end street.

God is calling to each of us saying, "Give me thine heart; I am thy King; let me rule; my kingdom is thy home." Recognizing this claim Ignatius put it

37

this way, "I come from God—I belong to God—I am destined for God."

In the second place, if we are to be followers of the King, we must seek to bring the culture of the mother country to this new land. To truly colonize, the culture, ideals, ways, codes of the mother country must be firmly planted in the new land. Her flag must be unfurled on the land. This means that our standards of life must come from the heavenly realm and hold sway in our lives here and now. The culture of heaven must become the culture of earth.

Our traditions, our way of life, our national heritage, our customs, our prejudices—all must be judged by God's judgments. This calls for adventure and often times misunderstanding. This is where it hurts. Following God's ways means that at times we break company with the ways of the world. Henry D. Thoreau put it this way: "If a man does not keep pace with his companions, perhaps it is because he hears a different drummer." Ours is a different drummer.

So, if we are to be true colonists of heaven here on earth, continually we must seek to bring the laws and ways of God's kingdom to bear on earth. Now we see that only as this is done can man survive the atomic age. Thomas Kelly puts it this way: "No average goodness will do, no measuring of our lives by our fellows, but only a relentless inexorable divine standard. No relatives will suffice; only absolutes satisfy the soul committed to holy obedience."

And finally, if we are to be true colonists of heaven, we must have frequent communication with the king of heaven. There is no substitute for this communication with Christ if we are to live as one of his. Temporarily we may neglect his presence, but sooner or later we discover that we must come back. Prayer and worship become then the very life-line of Christian power. When this supply-line is cut, then reinforcements cease to flow. The Christian who does not pray soon looses his Christian faith.

Someone has well said this about real worship. "It opens the avenue of the interior life and lets the spiritual currents from beyond us flow in and circulate about the roots of our being." It is those spiritual currents that keep us in touch with the King.

AIDS TO WORSHIP

HYMNS: "This Is My Father's World"
          "Guide Me, O Thou Great Jehovah"
SCRIPTURE: Phil. 3:16-21

A PRAYER

Our Father, who bestowest thy mercy at all times on them that love thee, and in no place art distant from those that serve thee, help us to know that though we take the wings of the morning and fly to the uttermost parts of the sea, lo, thou art there.

On every hand we see thy glory—in the beauty of thy creation, in the laughter of little children, in the songs of birds. In the love we have for one another, we come to know thee. Our Father, as we know thee, help us to serve thee, and in serving thee to love thee.

We would ask thy blessing upon this our native land. Guide and protect her during these days. Give integrity to those in authority, and help us to know that without thy power and thy wisdom the ship of state will be wrecked upon the dangerous shoals of wickedness and evil ways.

We are grateful for national independence and would forever be reminded of the price paid for it. But, O God, we seek an independence of spirit that frees us from becoming victim to life's evil temptations. We know that an independence of spirit comes only to those who depend upon thee, who seek thy way and thy will. Take us and use us in Christ's name. AMEN.

7
Religion—a faith, a task, a hope

Three college students walked up to Harry Emerson Fosdick after he had spoken on their campus and asked him this question: "What is the use of religious faith anyway?" It is a good question and ought to be answered, for we hear a great deal about religion today.

There are three elements in all religions, and they are faith, task, and hope. We are, of course, thinking today about our Christian religion which sees in Jesus Christ our clue to what God is like. Therefore, when we consider these three elements, we will be doing so from the Christian point of view.

The first of these elements is faith, a faith in some power upon whom man is dependent, and from whom he may expect help. This faith is basic and acknowledges the existence of God who is not dependent upon our ideas of him, but who is from everlasting to everlasting. He alone is one upon whom all truth depends, and without whom nothing else would exist. He is the absolute and sole God. He is the source of all being and the ruler of all history.

Upon him man depends for life and the strength of his days. From him man can expect help. His purposes for the world are being realized through man, but also in spite of man's evil and wickedness. He is the ruler of all history.

Jesus calls us to a faith in God as we know him in Christ, and when we respond to that call life takes on newer and richer meaning. A. D. Lindsay in his *Moral Teachings of Jesus* says, "When you get great religion, the religion which makes the world a different place and makes men do miracles, you find men deeply aware of their own littleness and impotence and proclaiming the majesty and sovereignty of God."

In the second place, there is another element in all religion, not only a faith, but also a task. It is a task to serve him and to worship him. It is a task to respond to his love for us by giving our love to him. Indeed, he is a jealous God, for his demands upon us are unconditional. We shall have no other gods before him.

Bernard Iddings Bell says in *Religion for Living*

The difference between the religious man and the magician is simple but profound. The magician seeks to get into contact with God in order to force, or induce, or persuade God to do or get for him, the magician, what he has no wit or power to do or get for himself; the religious man seeks to get into contact with God in order to find out what, in terms of a given situation, God expects him, the worshipper, to be and do, and to procure from God the strength and courage to perform the divine will.

There is a story told of a man who one day came to Whistler, the artist, asking for help in arranging a picture for a certain room. The man complained that the painting did not fit the room. Whereupon, the great artist replied, "Man, you're beginning at the wrong end. You can't make the painting fit the room. You will have to make the room fit the painting." So, when we look at God through Christ we can't make him fit into this sordid world or into our little lives, but we must make the world and ourselves fit into him and his way. We must make the room fit him.

We find a clue to the task or duty we owe to God in Micah 6:8. "He hath shewed thee, O man, what is good; and what doth the Lord require of thee, but to do justly, and to love mercy, and to walk humbly with thy God."

Finally, the third element in religion is hope. We want to know that our God is one who never lets up, who never lets down, and who never lets go. Sometimes we feel that he does weary of us and lets us down—especially when trouble comes. But then we remember that he has never promised to save us completely from trouble. To be sure there is trouble we may be spared by following him and by accepting his way, and not bucking his laws. But following him is no insurance policy against it. No one can look at the life of Jesus nor at Paul and believe that. We face trouble, disappointment, sorrow, heartache, and death as Christians.

But God has promised to save us in trouble. His strength enables us to see it through. To the burdened he says: "Come unto me, all ye that labour and are heavy laden, and I will give you rest." To the fearful he says: "Fear not: for, behold, I bring you good tidings of great joy." To the lonely he says: "Lo, I am with you alway even unto the end of the world." To the bereaved he says: "Let not your heart be troubled." To the bored he says: "I am come that they might have life, and that they might have it more abundantly." To us all he says: "My peace I give unto you: not as the world giveth, give I unto you. Let not your heart be troubled, neither let it be afraid."

Then, it is our hope that he never lets us go. He is unwearied in his search for the souls of men. In Deuteronomy we have these words: "For the Eternal . . . will not let you go" (Moffatt). And as Walt Whitman puts it: "Not until the sun refuses to shine do I refuse you."

Faith then is not merely our holding on to God, but it is also God holding on to us. This is our hope.

"Behold, I stand at the door, and knock: if any man hear my voice, and open the door, I will come in to him, and will sup with him, and he with me."

AIDS TO WORSHIP

Hymns: "Rise Up, O Men of God"
          "O Master, Let Me Walk with Thee"
Scripture: Isa. 40:26-31

A PRAYER

Eternal God, in whom we live and move and have our being, we come before thee this day unworthy of thy love. We come stained by temptations which so easily best us. We come feeling need of thee, thy power, thy strength, and thy forgiveness.

Thou knowest us better than we know ourselves; thou knowest our needs, and thou hast promised to help us if we but turn to thee. Take us this day and lift us upward. Strengthen our steps, enlarge our visions, quicken our hopes, purify our motives. Remind us of the things which do not change and secure us to life's unfading treasures, through Jesus Christ our Lord. AMEN.

8

More bridges needed

Bridges have always had a fascination for me. They have been wonderful aids to mankind serving as connecting links, spans that unite. When the Brooklyn Bridge was built in 1883 hurling its 1,595½ feet of heavy steel across the East River, it was hailed as an engineering miracle which would serve the transporation needs of many generations between Manhattan and Brooklyn. But as traffic increased, the narrow lanes became inadequate. Newer bridges were required.

So in 1903 the Williamsburg Bridge with its 1,600 feet of metal soon answered the growing need. But still that was not enough, so in 1909 the Queensboro Bridge with 1,182 feet was added, and soon the Manhattan Bridge of 1,470 feet joined the other two. But even this did not meet the crying needs, and to ease the congested traffic the Hell Gate Bridge of 977½ feet was added in 1917, and the 1,380-foot Triborough Bridge in 1936. But even with these six bridges totaling 8,205 feet, the problem was not solved. What a wonderful purpose these bridges have served through the years.

There are many interesting bridges: the George Washington Bridge over the beautiful Hudson River in New York; the Cooper River Bridge in Charleston; the London Bridge in London; the Ponte Vecchio across the Arno River in Florence, Italy; the lovely bridge in the Magnolia Gardens in Charleston, and many others. These not only serve a purpose of connecting but also add beauty to the areas surrounding them.

But many of these bridges no longer adequately serve the crowded conditions of modern cities and have to be supplanted by other bridges and tunnels. Equally great is the growing need for more bridges of brotherhood and understanding as the human traffic increases. As life becomes more congested, more bridges will be needed.

There was a guild in southern France during the twelfth century which was called "Bridge Building Brothers." It was made up of nobles, clergymen, and artisans, and was approved by Pope Clement III in A.D. 1191. The purpose of this guild was to clear difficult and dangerous roads, to assist pilgrims, and to build all sorts of bridges over rivers, brooks, treacherous precipices, and dangerous ravines.

In a real sense this guild could well describe Christians, for we should all be bridge building brothers. For one thing, our leader, Jesus Christ, was himself a bridge between heaven and earth. It is he that we worship. Paul said, "God was in Christ, reconciling the world unto himself." He gives us our clue to the

47

nature of God. In him we know what God is like. In him we find the near end of God.

And like Jesus, we who are his followers should be something of a bridge leading men to God. Jesus left for us our marching orders when he said, "Go ye therefore, and teach all nations, baptizing them in the name of the Father, and of the Son, and of the Holy Ghost." Had it not been for human beings the chances are you and I would never have known of the love of God.

This leads us to this thought: men will find in us that which reflects the nature of God when they find love and kindness in us. It is true what Julia Carney once wrote in her poem *Little Things*.

> Little deeds of kindness, little words of love,
> Help to make earth happy like the heaven above.

The poem, *The Bridge Builder*, gives us a beautiful closing thought on the part you and I are to play. You recall how an old man, who had crossed a sullen stream at evening, turned and built a bridge across the chasm he had just safely passed. A bystander asked him why, as he would never pass that way again. Here is his answer:

> The builder lifted his old gray head;
> "Good friend, in the path I have come," he said,
> "There followed after me to-day
> A youth whose feet must pass this way.
> This chasm that has been as naught to me

48

To that fair-haired youth may a pitfall be;
He, too, must cross in the twilight dim;
Good friend, I am building this bridge for him!"
—Will Allen Dromgoole

AIDS TO WORSHIP

HYMNS: "Lord, Speak to Me, That I May Speak"
          "Take My Life, and Let It Be"
SCRIPTURE: II Cor. 5:17-21

A PRAYER

O thou eternal God, in whom we live and move and have our being, with thankful hearts we praise thy holy name.

This is thy world, and we are thy children living in the Father's house. But we bow before thee in shame because we have not lived as kindred one with another. Our selfishness and pride have separated us, our prejudice has divided us. We have not loved one another as thou hast willed that we should. Forgive us for our unbrotherly ways.

We come too confessing our sin in thinking too highly of ourselves. We know that we are weak and frail beings in great need of a Redeemer and Savior who can lift us out of our sordid selves. We have done those things which we ought not to have done and left undone those things which we ought to have done.

So, we come to thee in need of the Christ who is the Savior of the world and who alone can save us from sin. Take us this day and make us more worthy servants of thine, through Jesus Christ, our Lord, we pray. AMEN.

49

9
Life's healing power

    Immediately after Jesus was baptized by John, he went into the desert to remain for forty days and there be tempted and tested. Mark says Jesus "was in the company of wild beasts; and the angels ministered unto him."

Mark alone mentions the wild beasts, and for him they serve either to intensify the loneliness of the wilderness or to typify the strong merciless character of the forces of evil.

The angels may very well symbolize the forces of righteousness and purity ever present in the arena of the soul's struggle. They may represent to us today life's healing powers at work in God's world. Certainly when we reflect upon life's uncertainties and evils, we can see certain forces that minister to our need.

Healing powers are at our disposal in the physical world. Let us look at this force which we may call life's healing power at work in the realm of plant life. Look at trees where limbs have been severed, and soon we will discover a protective covering that heals the wounds of that tree.

Perhaps in animal life the healing powers of life are more evident to us, for it is where we live. Broken fingers to broken backs are healed. When we get a wound on our bodies, immediately there are forces within the body which start their healing functions. It is amazing to witness this power at work.

One of the leading physicians in America, who has performed hundreds of autopsies, claims that a large proportion of human ills are cured before the victims even know they had the affliction. Proof was found that the healing forces had quietly done their work without being specially called in.

Dr. Alexis Carrel in his book *Man, the Unknown*, referring to the properties of blood, says, "Blood carries to each tissue the proper nourishment, but acts, at the same time, as a sewer that takes away the waste products set free by living tissues. It also contained chemical substances and cells capable of repairing organs wherever necessary."

Every decade witnesses new medical discoveries and new drugs which help to prolong life. Yet, after doctors and nurses have done all they can, they must in the final analysis rely on life's healing powers to mend their patient.

The father of French surgery in the sixteenth century, Ambroise Paré, had these words inscribed over the door of a hospital in Paris: "I dress the wound; God heals it."

51

After being confronted with many kinds of diseases, a woman said, "With all the germs there are and the diseases that threaten man, I do not see how we are ever well." A wise doctor answered her by saying, "Knowing the human body as I do, I do not see why a person is ever sick."

But there is another area of life no less real and in reality more important than the physical world, and that is this power at work in the spiritual realm. It is at work when a loved one dies. How unbearable seem the hours! Life seems to hold no meaning for the future. But gradually and surely this healing power helps us to withstand and carry on. It heals our inner wounds. When we are afraid, this power will give us courage. When we are lonely, this power gives us comfort. When our spirits sin and wander into a far country, this power is still at work to heal our wounds. The Prodigal's return was this power at work. Sometimes we call it conscience, but in reality it is God at work.

Now this power at work in the world of nature—in plant life, animal life, social progress, and spiritual life—is one and the same power. It is God at work in his world. It is a personal power that touches us where we live. It is a power that would save us in all areas of life.

[He] "was with the wild beasts; and the angels ministered unto him."

AIDS TO WORSHIP

HYMNS: "O Master, Let Me Walk with Thee"
            "My Faith Looks Up to Thee"
SCRIPTURE: Mark 1:1-13

A PRAYER

Eternal God, in whom we live and move and have our being, we give thee our gratitude for life's healing powers. We know that, as thou hast made us, it is within thy power to restore life when in need of repair.

We are thankful for all thy servants who do thy bidding in ministering to the broken bodies of men. We are grateful for the tender concern, the skilled hands and trained minds of nurses who give of themselves in dedicated service. We thank thee for doctors whose long years of study bring a healing ministry to those in distress. We are grateful for the generosity of many who have given of their substance that institutions of healing may bring aid to the sick in mind and body. We thank thee for friends and loved ones who watch beside beds of pain, and for all who offer prayers to thee for recovery. In their ministries we feel something of thy concern for our lives, and we are grateful, through Jesus Christ, our Lord. AMEN.

10

Life begins from within

We all know how difficult it is to be genuinely Christian today. Someone has said that unless we have that within us which is above us we shall become like that around us. "What's the use in trying to be Christian in a world like this?" is a question we often hear asked by men today, and there is something in what they say. It is terribly difficult, but that is not the whole truth. The fact is we can be Christian in spite of everything.

Here is Paul from a prison cell in Rome writing to his beloved Philippians, "All the saints salute you, chiefly they that are of Caesar's household." Imagine "saints in Caesar's household!" Of all places where one would least expect to find saints would be in such a household. Yet in spite of such a pagan environment they remained Christian.

Well, the world today, which is very much like Caesar's household, needs followers of the way who are saints. God needs men today who have depth of power and consecration of purpose. Times like these call for bigness of spirit, warmth of heart, overflowing love.

But we do not become sufficient or adequate for times like these unless we have inner resources to offset this outer world's pressure upon us. Although it may be hostile, bitter, and even at times unbearable, our inner world can meet it with poise, confidence, and trust. There was Paul living valiantly in the inner world while the outer was crumbling. Can you not see him there in Rome sending his messages of hope and cheer through prison bars to his beloved Philippians? There was St. Augustine writing his immortal *City of God* in days when the Roman Empire was falling, and the whole earth shaking. What can be true of characters like these can be true of us in our commonplace experiences. Where we live and work we can be saints in Caesar's household.

Elizabeth Barrett Browning hinted at the secret when she wrote "Life Develops from Within." And Douglas Steere has given testimony to this same truth in his stimulating little book, *Beginning from Within.*

How we do need spiritual adequacy today—goodness to offset evil! George Buttrick has reminded us that there is simply not enough goodness in the world to go around, and, if there is to be more goodness, it must come from the source of all goodness —God.

Henry Sloan Coffin gives us a meaningful definition of religion when he says that religion is not primarily doing good nor being good, but being connected with someone that makes what you do better than you could do by yourself, and makes what you are better than you could be by yourself.

Ethel Barrymore, the celebrated actress, found need of this connection with that someone. After living through dark years of defeat and failure, she made a triumphant comeback and was asked one day to give her own philosophy of living. She replied, "I suppose the greatest thing in the world is loving people and . . . wanting to destroy the sin, but not the sinner. And not to forget that when life knocks you to your knees, which it always does and always will—well, that's the best position in which to pray, isn't it? On your knees. That's where I learned."

And it is on our knees that we will become spiritually adequate for so great a need. Travelers to Copenhagen tell us that when you enter the cathedral to see Thorwaldsen's statue of Christ you will not be able to see his face unless you kneel at his feet. With outstretched arms he looks down upon all those who are looking up. So, if as Christians we are to be adequate for times like these, at his feet we must begin our quest.

AIDS TO WORSHIP

HYMNS: "Dear Lord and Father of Mankind"
  "Holy Spirit, Faithful Guide"
SCRIPTURE: Phil. 4:13-23

A PRAYER

Eternal God, thou hast been our dwelling place in all generations; thou art our refuge and strength. With grateful hearts we praise thee this day.

We thank thee for thy watchful care during the darkness of the night. We know that thou art ever near to guide and to guard. Even when we are unaware of it, thy love reaches out to us and blesses us.

Here this day we rest our fears in thy keeping, and we are not afraid of what life may bring to us. With thee as our companion and friend, we know that we are never alone.

But we do confess that at times we loose the consciousness of thy presence and wander for from home. And at times we question whether life is worth living, and yet in our better moments we know that it is— when we follow thy way. Help us know that thou art always waiting to receive us back again. When we are bewildered by decisions which are hard to make, be for us a light unto our path, for we need thy wisdom here.

Give us this day a clearer grasp of the things which belong unto our peace and a closer walk with him who is the source of our peace. Through Jesus Christ, our Lord, we pray. AMEN.

II

Gratitude heals a broken heart

All of us find ourselves at one time or another faced with sorrow and grief. What can we do when we lose those we love?

There are three things to suggest. *First, let us remember that life is a fragile thing, and that we all soon follow those who slip from our midst.*

Addison in his *Meditations in Westminster Abbey* has a word of comfort for us:

"When I look upon the tombs of the great, every emotion of envy dies in me; when I read the epitaphs of the beautiful, every inordinate desire goes out; when I meet with the grief of parents upon a tombstone, my heart melts with compassion; when I see the tombs of the parents themselves, I consider the vanity of grieving for those whom we must quickly follow; when I see kings lying by those who deposed them, when I consider rival wits placed side by side, or the holy men that divided the world with their contests and disputes, I reflect with sorrow and astonishment on the little competitions, factions, and debates of mankind."

So, remembering that we follow those who leave us and through our faith can look forward to a blessed reunion brings a measure of comfort to us.

Again, to busy ourselves with work can help us through the valley of sorrow. The other day a friend of mine who had lost a young son through a dreadful accident, said this to me, "You know, after Jerry was killed, my husband and I busied ourselves with our work. We visited our people from morning till night, and sharing their problems helped us with ours. I don't know how we would have gotten through those days had it not been for our work." How many people have had the anguish of sorrow lessened by work!

Finally, it is through gratitude that we find our best antidote for sorrow. Even in the midst of our tears we can discover so much for which we have to be grateful. Dwelling here helps to heal our wounds.

Recently, where there had been long illness and suffering, a loved one who had been standing by in tender care said, "I know I have so much to be thankful for. And it is in remembering God's mercy and blessings that has helped me stand these days." How true this is!

Whether we are faced with bereavement, disappointment, or joy, let us make it a habit to be grateful to God for his boundless love and goodness expressed in our lives in so many ways. It is good to "count our many blessings, name them one by one." Gratitude lights a lonely way. Gratitude helps to heal a broken heart.

Shakespeare put it like this: "God's goodness hath been great to thee. Let never day nor night unhallowed pass, but still remember what the Lord hath done."

A person confessed that he would never forget the beauty and serenity that possessed the life of his grandmother. Her long years were fraught with many trials and tribulations, but her life was like a song. Always in her heart and frequently upon her lips were these words of the Psalmist: "Bless the Lord, O my soul: and all that is within me, bless his holy name. Bless the Lord, O my soul, and forget not all his benefits."

AIDS TO WORSHIP

HYMNS: "Saviour, Like a Shepherd Lead Us"
          "Lord, for Tomorrow and Its Needs"
SCRIPTURE: Ps. 63:1-7

A PRAYER

O thou eternal one, Father and Comforter of all men, draw especially near to all whose hearts are filled with sadness over the loss of a loved one. Beyond their tears help them to know there is life that shall never end. In their sadness help them know that thou dost understand. In their loneliness make them conscious of thy great love. In their grief draw them closer unto thee.

Help them to bear bravely the anguish of these hours. Fill the vacancy of their hearts with thy abiding presence, which links us to those who pass beyond. Grant that we may rest our fears in thy hands trusting in thy promises and waiting for the day when we shall be joined together in thy eternal home, through Jesus Christ, our Lord. AMEN.

12

God's angry men

In the fifth verse of the third chapter of Mark we read: "And he looked around at them with anger" (R.S.V.). In this passage we find that Jesus was angered at the hardness of the hearts of those who watched to see if he would heal the man with the withered hand on the Sabbath day.

Now anger is a strong word, and yet, Halford E. Luccock says no other will do, for Jesus had his moments of anger. There are those who take occasion to criticize him for being angry, but in Jesus' case to be angry was not so much a human failing as a human endowment. He had the capacity of righteous indignation.

It has been said that all great virtues are the result of two moral forces pulling in opposite directions. For example, love degenerates unless it is balanced by the capacity for righteous indignation. Without the abhorrence of evil, kindness becomes undiscriminating.

Harry Emerson Fosdick points out that the great Indian religions preach love and goodwill. For example, a Buddhist saint sits in seclusion contemplating goodwill toward all creation. He loves all men, good and evil, but he never lifts his finger to help a person, nor to be concerned over the evils of his land.

A follower of Christ loves also, but to him love means also to abhor evil. He hates the system that causes the downfall of young girls in a vicious traffic. He resents the apathy which leaves millions without education in our world. A good Christian is a man of wrath and has heard the injunction of Paul: "Ye that love the Lord hate evil."

Now let us look and see some of the things which caused Jesus to be angry.

Let us remember that he was never angry at a private wrong. His indignation was never brought about by any wrong done to him as an individual. He said in Matthew 12:32, "Whosoever speaketh a word against the Son of man, it shall be forgiven him."

This freedom from all personal resentment by one who had such capacity for indignation is really beyond our understanding of ordinary human nature. George Matheson confessed: "There are times when I do well to be angry, but I have mistaken the times." On another occasion Jesus in the agony of death cried out, "Father, forgive them; for they know not what they do" (Luke 23:34).

But Jesus was profoundly stirred when someone hurt another. He was moved to anger when the Pharisees elevated their own self-interest and tradi-

63

tion above humanity and failed to apprecaite human values. Here in their midst a man was in need, and that seemed to mean nothing to them compared to their own rigid tradition of keeping the Sabbath day. Jesus blazed with anger. He was angry whenever there was an elevation of any privilege or gain above human need. When property values outranked human need, we may well remember that Jesus looked around at them with anger.

But let us remember that his condemnation was balanced by his appreciation of the good he saw. Condemnation alone accomplishes nothing.

There is an old Persian legend which illustrates Jesus' appreciation of life:

Jesus arrived one evening at the gates of a certain city and sent his disciples forward to prepare supper, while he himself, intent on doing good, walked through the streets into the market-place. He saw at the corner of it some people gathered together looking at an object on the ground, and he drew near to see what it might be. It proved to be a dead dog, with a halter around its neck, by which it appeared to have been dragged through the dirt, and a viler, a more abject, a more unclean thing, never met the eyes of man. "Faugh," said one, stopping his nose, "it pollutes the air." "How long," said another, "shall this foul beast offend our sight?" "Look at his torn hide," said a third, "one could not even cut a shoe out of it." "And his ears," said a fourth, "all draggled and bleeding." "No doubt," said a fifth," he has been hanged for thieving." And Jesus heard them, and looking down compassionately on the dead creature, he said, "Pearls cannot equal the whiteness of his teeth." And the people turned toward him in amazement, and said among themselves, "Who is this? This must be Jesus of Nazareth, for who else could find anything to pity or approve in a dead dog?" And being ashamed they bowed their heads before him, and went on their way.

Now let us ask ourselves, "What angers us?"

Do we become angry over that which affects us personally, or over injustices to people and indifference to human need? Can we look unconcerned at vast human suffering or wrong, or be complacent as long as it does not touch us, only to flame with anger over slights, real or imagined, over threats to our prestige, our vanity, our comfort, our pocketbooks?

Surely in our world there is a real need today for God's angry men—men who are angered at wrong done others, at systems and traffics which endanger human life, and at any privilege which is gained at the price of another.

How grateful we should be to know that the God we worship, as we discover him in Christ, is one who has the capacity for anger and who throws his weight on the side of righteousness, honesty, and goodness.

AIDS TO WORSHIP

HYMNS: "Come, thou Almighty King"
           "He Leadeth Me"

SCRIPTURE: Matt. 5:1-12

A PRAYER

O most merciful and righteous God, into thy holy presence we come this day with praise upon our lips and thanksgiving in our hearts. Through countless ages thou hast ruled this thy world. In every generation thou art concerned in it still.

Here in this place we feel thy presence near, and we open our minds and hearts to the leadership of thy spirit. Some of us, our Father, are weaker than others, but all of us need thy power and thy strength to make us strong. The temptations which daily confront us try our spirits. We find ourselves doing those things which we ought not to do and leaving undone those things which we ought to do. Take us this day and make us worthy servants of thine. In Christ's name, we pray. Amen.

13
Here is the secret

Traveling through the mountains of western North Carolina a man came to a section of the highway which was under repair. It was necessary for traffic to take a one-way route over that part of the highway. Along with other motorists he was stopped by a flagman. They waited until the southbound line of cars came through. Then the driver of the last car gave a flag to his flagman indicating that the road was clear and that they could go through.

This is really a parable about life. How dependent we are upon those who travel before us for some word about the journey ahead. In many sections our road is a narrow way with only one-way traffic, and we need a word from those who have traveled it. We need a flag to tell us "all clear, you can travel now!"

Paul, whose life had been filled with hardships and trial, says, "In any and all circumstances I have learned the secret of facing plenty and hunger, abundance and want." Then he hands us this secret; he gives us that flag: "I can do all things in him who strengthens me" (R.S.V.). He is saying that with Christ the road is safe! He tells us two things wherein he has found it to be so.

For one thing, he says that when life favors us with plenty, Christ is our secret in handling it. How many times success and happiness become for us danger moments when we forget God, and when we depend upon our own resources to see us through.

In our favored situation we can become arrogant, conceited, and self-satisfied. We need more than ever to rest our dependence upon God, as many a person, intoxicated with success, has forgotten God and his demands and thereby missed the way.

There is an old adage which says, "Success may separate us from our neighbors, but trouble makes kinsfolk of us all." Not only can success separate us from our neighbors, but it can also separate us from God. That is why we need Christ when life favors us. He makes us humble and above all grateful for life and its joys.

A second thing Paul is telling us is that in the circumstance of hunger or want he has learned the secret of living. In other words, he is saying when life treats us hard, when hardships come, when trouble invades our homes, when sorrow overtakes us—even then through Christ we can face it. He gives us the strength to see it through.

So, when you are in want and despair, remember this flag Paul handed down from years of travel over the same rugged highway of life, over disappointment, sorrow, hardship—passing it on to you and me—saying even in want you can win victory through Christ.

What a comforting and challenging thought it is! When so much of our life is lived in trouble, just to know that God helps us bear it, this is one of the great secrets of living, available to everyone. Depend upon him, trust him to see you through. Go out each day with a confidence that God through Christ goes with you. Go knowing that with this flag of assurance nothing can happen that can really hurt you.

To possess this faith and to live by it is one of life's greatest possessions. It alone can take away the fear which is hounding you, which robs your days of radiance and joy. It alone can bring into your life a serenity and peace which the world cannot take away. "I know how to be abased, and I know how to abound; in any and all circumstances I have learned the secret of facing plenty and hunger, abundance and want. I can do all things in him who strengthens me" (R.S.V.).

AIDS TO WORSHIP

HYMNS: "I Am Thine, O Lord"
  "O Jesus, I Have Promised"
SCRIPTURE: Phil. 4:8-13

A PRAYER

O thou eternal God, who hast given us the breath of life and who hast ordained that we should be useful in thy kingdom's building, help us to see afresh thy way and thy purpose for our lives.

What we want is to do thy will and to fulfill thy plan. Grant that the lure of the market place and the temptations that daily confront us may not steer us from that course. We know that thy plan and thy will is best for us. But sometimes it is so hard for us to follow it. So, here today we are asking for strength to do the right and insight into what it is.

We are thankful that thou dost not expect the impossible from us, but only that we do the best we can with what we have. Help us begin now to start being our best.

We praise thee, we worship thee, we glorify thee who art forever and ever. AMEN.

14
Getting along with people

One of the most important things we have to learn is to get along with people. We are social beings and on every hand relate ourselves to others, and unless we learn to live peaceably with all kinds of people life will be bitter and hard.

We are told that Andrew Carnegie paid Charles Schwab the unprecedented salary of one million dollars a year. It was not that Schwab knew more about steel than the men under him. He confessed himself that many of his men knew far more about steel than he did. But he was paid such a salary because of his ability to deal with people. Andrew Carnegie was willing to pay over three thousand dollars a day to a man who knew how to get along with people.

We, too, have known men who were well qualified, yet not able to work well with others, and, consequently, they failed.

Now, being able to get along does not mean necessarily that one is agreeable to everything that happens. Not at all. There is a way to disagree without being disagreeable, to stand for principle without stirring up a cyclone, to have convictions without being obnoxious. To be sure there may come a time or situation in which a person will break step with others and in so doing gain their disapproval and even enmity.

But we must cultivate the art of relating ourselves happily to other people without sacrificing principle and conviction. Let us consider some practical suggestions as we seek to cultivate this art.

In the first place, we should learn to differ without getting angry. This is one of the hardest things we have to do. There are people who simply cannot tolerate any disagreement. They take such as a personal attack which, of course, makes it hard to get along with others. Those who work under them hesitate to offer suggestions for fear they would cut across their plans and bring forth their wrath. The chances are that such people are unsure of themselves, which makes them hold fast to their own notions lest they lose stature.

Learning to differ without being disagreeable is to recognize that no one has all the answers or the whole truth. It is to be teachable. An "I-want-my-own-way" attitude will never do.

After Gladstone died, the widow of the great statesman discovered in his private papers a long list of names which bore the title, "Those who have disagreed with me." Below were penned these words in Gladstone's handwriting: "Good for me to remember what notable people have differed with me."

Then, too, the person who gets along is one who is sincerely interested in what is happening to others. Rather than bore others with the details of his own operation, he inquires with real interest into the details of theirs.

I know a lady who has had few advantages in life. She lives in a small community and is married to a man whose income is very modest. She has never been to college, but people who have go to her for advice. They like to be around this lady because of her genuine concern in what is happening to them.

Do you remember the story of the egotist who having spent most of an evening talking about himself suddenly stopped and said, "That's enough about me. Let's hear about you. For instance, how did you like my new book?"

This interest in other people goes down deeper than surface concern or an interest based on a selfish motive. *It is based on a deep respect for personality.* It sees people as ends, of great value within themselves, and never as means to some selfish, personal end.

Tolstoi was one who felt deeply with people and for them. One day he passed a beggar who had asked for alms. Tolstoi reached in his pockets but found no money. Then he walked up to the beggar and embraced him, saying apologetically, "Do not be angry with me, little brother, because I have nothing to give you." The face of the beggar began to glow and as great tears ran down his cheeks he whispered:

73

"But, sir, you called me brother, that was a great gift."

A third suggestion is: *Take your share of the load and be willing to give the other fellow credit for his.*

There are some people who are always ready to lead but never to follow. They want to be forever in the limelight, and unless they are, they will not play the game. They are willing to give but not to take orders. Longfellow once said, "The talent of success is nothing more than doing what you can well, and doing whatever you do without any thoughts of fame." Another has well said that there is no telling the amount of good one person can do if he is not too interested in who gets the credit.

One of the real marks of Lincoln's greatness was revealed in an order which he sent a commanding officer during the war. The Battle of Gettysburg had just been fought, and Lincoln sensed an opportunity to end the war. As commander-in-chief of the Union forces, he ordered General Meade to pursue. To his orders he attached these instructions in the President's handwriting: "The note I enclose is not of record. If you succeed, you need not reveal it. If you fail, publish it. Then, if you succeed, you will have all the credit of the movement. If not, I'll take all the responsibility."

AIDS TO WORSHIP

HYMNS: "Come Thou Fount of Every Blessing"
           "Where Cross the Crowded Ways of Life"

SCRIPTURE: 1 John 3:1-11

A PRAYER

O God from whose hands come life's gifts and through whose servants we are blessed, grant that we may ever be aware of those who make life fuller for us. Forbid that we should accept their services without gratitude or that we should ever take them for granted. For countless thousands who daily minister to our needs we give thee hearty thanks:

For those who paint our houses and clean our walls, may their ladders hold firm and their scaffolds be steady;

For grocerymen who serve us food every day, grant unto them strength for long hours of toil and patience in handling details;

For the postman who brings us news in bad and good days, go with him in the daily round and sustain him under heavy loads;

For policemen keeping guard over our community, give unto them a sense of dignity in their work and through the long night-watches a consciousness of thy abiding presence;

For the doctor, bestow unto him unusual strength and health as he answers our calls of distress;

Through these and all thy servants our lives are made richer, and we give unto thee our gratitude for their ministries. AMEN.

15
The significance of the tiny

In a world of mass movements and glorification of the gigantic, it is well for us to remember the importance of little things. We have been prone to speak disparagingly of the individual's place in the world. We have often concluded that our help is only a drop in the bucket.

This feeling of inadequacy is not new. When Jesus suggested to the disciples that they feed the weary multitude, Andrew looked at Jesus with amazement, saying: "There is a lad here, which hath five barley loaves, and two small fishes: but what are they among so many?" The resources seemed so small for such a multitude.

Yet, we know how Jesus took what was at hand, a little basket of food, and answered the hunger of a crowd. You can imagine how little and insignificant the boy felt in the face of such need. The size of the problem and the meagerness of his resources made him feel a mere spectator, tempted to do nothing but watch. Then, to his amazement, Christ took what he had and made him, not a spectator, but a participant. He did matter after all. What he had was needed. His loaves and fishes did count.

So, let us remind ourselves of the significance of the minute, the tiny, and the dependence of big things upon little things. Let us consider the importance and place of little things in life. A casual meeting, a chance sentence, an accidental discovery— such have shaped history far out of proportion to their size and seeming significance.

When Thomas Jefferson was an old man telling about the final signing of the Declaration of Independence, he said that most of the members had planned to debate the matter at length before signing. But the day appointed was hot, and through the open doors of the Philadelphia Statehouse came a swarm of flies from a nearby stable. They made for the stockinged legs of the members, and in the confusion and discomfort all thought of debate was forgotten. Hurriedly, they signed the document which was to be the foundation of a new nation in America.

We see the significance of the tiny every day in nature if we have eyes open to God's world. A pound of honey is made up of 7,000 grains of sugar. To get this honey a bee must visit 56,000 clover heads, as each contains only one-eighth of a grain. Now a clover head has sixty flower tubes, so the bee must perform the extracting process 3,360,000 times to secure enough sweetness for one pound of honey.

Today little things have come into their own in science. The discovery of atomic energy has focused our attention upon the importance of the tiny. Robert Hutchins says that less than fifteen pounds of atomic fuel will produce enough energy for all the demands of the United States for one year. And one boxcar of atomic fuel will produce enough energy to heat every building, illuminate every electric bulb, and operate every machine in the entire world for a thousand years.

We find these words in Matthew 13:31-33:

"Another parable he put before them, saying, "The kingdom of heaven is like a grain of mustard seed which a man took and sowed in his field; it is the smallest of all seeds, but when it has grown it is the greatest of shrubs and becomes a tree, so that the birds of the air come and make nests in its branches."

He told them another parable. "The kingdom of heaven is like leaven which a woman took and hid in three measures of meal, till it was all leavened."

In these two parables we have words of encouragement and hope. The mustard seed is almost too small to be seen. It takes hundreds of them to make a gram. Yet, this is the seed that grows up into a great shrub, "and a fat sparrow, who has picked hundreds of these tiny seeds for his breakfast, can teeter on its branches."

Helmut Thielicke reminds us that Jesus in speaking of the mysterious growth of Christianity was "not thinking so much of the quantitative process by which his church grows ever larger and finally, in a mighty Christian invasion, conquers the continents and islands, but rather of the fact that in his church there is an indwelling dynamic which must lay hold upon everything around it."

This brings us to his use of the yeast, the "leaven" which leavens the whole mass of meal and changes its quality. And, as Thielicke says,

This is the point of the "salt," even the smallest quantity of which changes a whole plate of soup. This is the point of those sayings which speak of the church as a "light" in the world. How exceedingly small is the source of light in an auto headlight, and how tremendously great is the cone of light it cuts out of the gigantic darkness of a nocturnal landscape.

So, Jesus is saying that Christians, so far as numbers are concerned, are a small group, a minority; but he is saying that within that minority there is dynamic power which can alter life around it and which can change the whole world.

This leads us to the fact that if we are faithful in the little things in life the big things will take care of themselves. Within our Christian faith there is power to alter life.

If the seed is not planted, it will not grow into a big shrub. If the yeast is not put in the dough, it will not leaven it. If the light is kept under the basket, it will not cut through the darkness. To be faithful wherever we are—this is what Jesus is asking of us.

AIDS TO WORSHIP

HYMNS: "How Firm a Foundation"
          "My Hope Is Built on Nothing Less"
SCRIPTURE: Matt. 13:31-35

A PRAYER

O Thou Eternal God, who art beyond the reaches of our highest thoughts and yet who art within each one of us, we come before thee this day praising thy Holy Name.

On every hand we see thy handiwork—in the beauty of this day, in the joys of earthly companionship, in the laughter of little children, in the affection we have for one another. But especially, our Father, we see thee and know thee in Jesus Christ, our Lord. We remember his words, "He that hath seen me hath seen the Father." Help us to be more like him, to see in him the kind of person thou wouldst have us be. Give to us the consciousness of thy Holy Spirit which guides us and upholds us.

Send us forth to live at our best, through Jesus Christ, our Lord. AMEN.

16
Prove it by you

Several years ago a group of young people was asked what it means to be a Christian. One young girl ventured this answer, "To be a Christian is to live like Mr. Clemmer." She was saying that the greatest evidence of the proof of Christianity is the testimony of those who live by it. This was what Knox had in mind when he said, "The experience of those who lived by it was the fundamental proof of Christianity."

This goes for all truth. Truth remains theory until we see it exemplified in some actual life situation. Truth is abstract and often meaningless until it becomes personified in life. When truth moves men, it does so through a personal medium. Love is vague until we see it in a lover. Love is empty until we love or are loved. To be sure ideas may rule the world, but only through personality. Incarnate truth and truth comes alive.

Phillips Brooks once said the same thing in a little different way.

All truth must be brought, in order to be effective,

through a personal medium. Which of us can dare say that he would hold the most effective truths that he believes in just as much the same way as he does now, if they had come to him anonymously? . . . We have some personality behind them all; a mother's voice yet trembles in them, a father's authority makes them solemn, a teacher's enthusiasm will not let us count them trivial, and so they first have gained and they still hold their great power over us.

But there is a mood in our time, as Halford Luccock reminds us, which makes men say with a shrug of the shoulders, "Well, you can't prove it by me." To be sure there is a great deal in life we cannot prove, but the fact is people ought to be able to prove Christianity by us.

This is the story of the Christian church. Throughout history the world has only known what Christianity is when men and women demonstrated by their lives what it meant. Christianity captured the peoples of the first century by making known through those whose lives embraced it just what its meaning was.

"See how these Christians love one another," they said. And people joined the church before they accepted the ideas that the church held because of the love people had for one another.

When Jesus proclaimed the love of God and his tender care for all his sheep, people were attracted to his matchless teachings. But it was when he cared enough to give his life for that love that men really believed. Yes, when men have been confronted with the love of God revealed in the crucified Christ, they have said, "That's all I wanted to know."

We know Christianity is real, for we have seen God's love expressed through devoted friends and loved ones in hospitals. We have seen his love made real in the hearts of people concerned in the welfare of others. We have seen him walking here in houses of worship through the life of some devoted teacher or official. We have seen him expressing himself sacrificially when someone gave for others until it hurt. We have been witnesses to the fact that any man in Christ becomes a new creature. We have seen how faith energizes and cleanses life and how love has a saving way.

There are many whose lives bear witness to the proof of Christianity. There is a taxi driver in New York City, who repeats this prayer as he takes his taxi from the garage in the morning: "Lord, as I move through the streets of New York today, I am going to carry all kinds of people. Some will be happy, some will be worried, some will be suffering and broken. Lord, ride with me in my cab and help me to pass your healing spirit to everyone I meet." Yes, you could prove Christianity by him.

There was a man who died some years ago with an incurable disease. He lingered for many months and suffered untold pain. But what faith held him to his course. Always there was a calm confidence about him that one could never forget. You could prove Christianity by him.

Frequently there comes to mind the bent figure of my grandmother, who, regularly as the days came and went, would retire in the early morning to her room for prayer. I can hear her now praying out loud at times. I can see her coming from such moments renewed and strengthened for the day's toil. Yes, you could prove Christianity by her.

Proving your faith is not always done with verbal expression but many times in just living, just being— just walking, and not merely talking. You recall the Franciscan story which tells of how Francis on one occasion invited a young novice to accompany him on a preaching expedition through town, and how they passed through one street after another and eventually returned to their starting point and not a word had been spoken. "But Father," said the novice, puzzled and disappointed, "I thought we were going to preach?" "We have preached," replied Francis. "We were observed as we walked. They marked us as we went. It was thus we preached." Just simple living and walking in the faith is positive proof of the faith.

AIDS TO WORSHIP

HYMNS: "O Jesus, I Have Promised"
               "Be Strong"
SCRIPTURE: Ps. 1

A PRAYER

O God, we would know thee today, for this is the day that thou hast made. Help us to be joyous in it. Consecrate the experience of this day to thy service.

Grant that we may be kinder in our homes, more considerate in our business relationships, and more devoted to thy church. Help us to walk daily without fear, but with trust. Help us to follow the light of thy truth in dark places and to do right when it is so easy to do wrong.

Forgive us for our low moods when we should be joyous. Forgive us for the little sins which lay waste life when thy strength can enable us to overcome them. Control our pride which separates us from thee and grant that the misfortunes which come our way will lead us back to thee, through Jesus Christ, our Lord. AMEN.

17
Life's great adventure

There is a desire in the heart of every man for adventure. Whether it is in the life of a high school boy trying to thumb his way across country or a middle-aged woman trying to ride a horse for the first time, the experience of both is the same desire for adventure.

If we take a look in the bookstores, we will find that people are reading stories of adventure. If we go to the city library, the cards of patrons reveal that the thirst for adventure brings them back again and again. To those who frequent the theater, the crowds follow the movies of great stories of adventure.

Many people are only half living today. There are all the rich capacities of mind and soul with which they are endowed, but they are unused, silent, unproductive. Have you ever felt that way about some person—planned on a grand scale with unlimited possibilities and yet never getting beyond the actuality of today?

We find Jesus constantly looking into the faces of people of his day whom he knew had resources which were silent and unfruitful. He had the ability to look beyond the mere exterior of a person and bring forth the best that was within. Wherever he went, he created the desire in men to find themselves and become that type of person he talked about.

You recall the meeting of Jesus in the opening chapter of the Fourth Gospel with Simon Peter, the fisherman. When Jesus saw him he looked beyond the mere exterior of this crude fisherman and saw there the picture of a man of vast undeveloped resources. What he saw caused him to say, "Thou art Simon . . . : [but] thou shalt be called Cephas" (meaning Peter). "Thou art—what?" If he had filled it in he might have said, "Thou art Simon, a crude, unlettered fisherman. Thou art impulsive, arrogant, self-centered, and fickle. Thou art weak, unfaithful, cowardly, and an untrue friend." And completing the equation he might have said, "But thou shalt be Peter, a rocklike character; thou shalt be a mighty preacher upon whom I shall build my church; thou shalt be a tower of strength, a martyr, and a true witness."

To change the actual "thou art" into the ideal "thou shalt be" is the high function of Jesus Christ. He did it for Simon Peter, a star which rose in obscurity and set in splendor, and has been doing it for men ever since. Here is the life of John Bunyan, a man claimed to have been the ring leader in all sorts of vice and ungodliness, and one who had few equals for cursing and swearing. This is the man who was changed by the power of Jesus into the author of

87

Pilgrim's Progress, which has been spiritual food for countless thousands.

Self-centeredness and selfishness led John Wesley into a life of despair in Georgia. Finally God touched his life in a little Moravian meetinghouse in Aldersgate Street, London. From that night on the spirit of Christ burned in his heart as he went up and down England ministering to the poor and helpless.

Just as in the life of Simon Peter, Jesus came into the lives of John Bunyan and John Wesley and transformed their potentialities into actualities. But in doing this Jesus did not free these men from the hardships of living nor the pains of dying. He has always shown men that life is something from which they cannot escape by some trick but must be faced and courageously met. Though he did not free them from the dangers of life, yet he did give them power to face life, as Baron von Hugel has said, "power to grasp life's nettle." Today his spirit still knocks at our doors urging us to attain the full stature of manhood in life's great adventure.

Let us take a look and see what Jesus did for Simon Peter and can do for us. *In the first place, when Jesus said, "Thou art Simon," he was looking into the face of Simon recognizing what he was.* He was facing the facts, however crude they may have been, and this was what he was asking Simon to do. He was saying, "Know thyself."

And this is what you and I must do. Our potentialities are limited by what we are today—our actualities. God does not want us to do what is impossible, to become what we cannot. What he is asking and expecting is that we reach the highest possible stature with what we have. We must realize that each of us has limitations of one kind or another. It is to say that we must accept ourselves for what we are and with what we have to work.

In the second place, Jesus placed before Simon a vision of his ideal. In saying "Thou shalt be called [Peter]," he threw the ideal of what he might become on the screen before him. What a tremendous thing happens to any man when a picture of his best self is flashed before him. It is then that his daily life is judged in terms of that better self, and his today is lived in terms of what he hopes to become tomorrow.

Not only did Simon have a vision of his best self flashed before him, but also the kindling power of Jesus was before him as an ideal. He projected himself into this ideal, and what he saw changed the whole course of his life.

In the third place, Jesus became a great friend who believed in him. In saying, "Thou shalt be Peter," he was expressing his faith in this future disciple. Jesus' believing in him made him believe in himself. How well do we know that merely to be singled out as a friend and comrade is often enough to remake a man.

Friendship is a great dynamic. When one finds a person for whose approval and welfare one lives, one has come upon one of the greatest motivating forces in life. If the inside stories of great lives could be told, it would be found that behind each success and achievement a friend was applauding and sharing in both joys and sorrows alike. A friend may help you find yourself, for a real comrade knows us better than we know ourselves.

Knowing thyself, having a worthy ideal, having friends that believe in you—such does help us find ourselves and realize our best. But here we come to a strange paradox. We can never find our lives by consciously striving to do so. We can never attain the full stature of manhood by seeking to do so.

This leads to a fourth consideration. Finding one's life is a by-product of losing it in a cause bigger than oneself. This is what Jesus meant when he said, "He that findeth his life shall lose it, but he that loseth his life for my sake shall find it." He knew this when he said, "Thou art Simon . . . thou shalt be called [Peter]." And in the same moment he offered Simon a cause in which he could lose himself. "Come follow me, lose yourself, give yourself, and I will make you fishers of men."

Across the years that same challenge comes to us clear and distinct above the noise of the world. So, if life's great adventure is to be fulfilled, we, too, must accept the challenge and lose ourselves in the cause, the object of which is to bring the reign of God in the hearts of individuals and ultimately in every human association. Will you let the Christ

look into your heart and say, "Thou art Simon . . .
[but] thou shall be called [Peter]."

AIDS TO WORSHIP

HYMNS: "What a Friend We Have in Jesus"
"Take My Life, and Let It Be"
SCRIPTURE: John 1:29-42

A PRAYER

Holy, holy, holy, Lord God Almighty, heaven and
earth are full of thy glory; glory be to thee, O Lord most
high. Help us, our Father, to rejoice today in thy
worship and find gladness in the singing of thy praises.

Enable us to step aside from the busy life of common
days and take thought of its meaning and its end. Grant
that Jesus Christ may become the companion of our
thoughts, so that his divine manhood may more and
more take root within our souls.

May the comfort of his presence bind up the wounds
of the brokenhearted and give renewed hope to the
grief-stricken. We would remember our loved ones in
far-off places. Guard and protect them we pray.

Forgive us for our failures of the past and strengthen
us for our opportunities of the future, through Jesus
Christ, our Lord. AMEN.

91

18
Life's unguarded frontier

(New Year's Day)

One of the exhilarating experiences of the New Year is the opportunity to forget the past and start over again. It is a time for stocktaking, for evaluating, for revamping, for redirecting, and for remapping. We close the books on an old year's experience and open another on a new.

The new year is an unguarded frontier which can be crossed without passport or baggage checking. No visa is needed at its borders. We can leave behind what we will. We can take with us what we want. To be sure, what happens in the New Year will be determined in a measure by what has happened in the year or years gone by.

George Stewart has put into words sentiment about this time of the year. He writes:

We are before another allotment of time, a new year with fresh, clean pages on which we must write a record with fingers damaged by all our yesterdays. For some, fingers are stiff with age, cramped with rheumatic pains, for others fingers have lost their cunning by negligence or have never gained skill because of lazy habit. Others must write with fingers scarred by accident, twisted by too many heavy burdens; still others must write with young fingers which have not yet learned the ways of toil and of life, fingers calloused or soft, young or old, serviceable or ineffective, hands that tell our character and our history as truly as our faces, our speech, or our hearts.[1]

And how appropriate are these words from the mind and heart of Paul. "Brethren, I count not myself to have apprehended: but this one thing I do, forgetting those things which are behind, and reaching forth unto those things which are before, I press toward the mark for the prize of the high calling of God in Christ Jesus."

Let us look into this passage as we move into the early days of this new year.

In the first place, it suggests to us to leave behind the baggage of past mistakes and errors. To be sure we must profit by the mistakes we make in trying to avoid them, but after we have done this, let us forget them. To continually brood over a wrong road taken or a wrong decision made robs a person of vitality needed for new roads and new loads ahead.

All of us have made mistakes and poor choices. How it hurts our pride to look back on them and to be forced to say, "Only if I had done differently."

[1] Used by permission of George Stewart.

We are thinking here not so much of sins we have committed, but of poor judgment we have exercised, of chances we let pass, of dreams we never followed, of opportunities we never took.

Here we might include all those mistakes which belong to our circumstances over which we have no control. It may be that we stopped school either by necessity or out of wrong choice. Or looking back now we see that the work we elected to do was really not our calling, that against our best judgment we followed something which never brought satisfaction. Then there may be those who feel that opportunity did not knock at their door as it did at some other's.

Paul seems to be saying here, after you have accepted the facts which cannot be altered, forget them. These things have happened and cannot be altered. Do the best you can with what you have. The string may be broken, but pick up the ends and see if they cannot be tied together again.

Frederick W. Robertson once said,

It is not by regretting what is irreparable that true work is to be done, but by making the best of what we are. It is not by complaining that we have not the right tools, but by using well the tools we have. . . . The manly and the wise way is to look your disadvantages in the face, and see what can be made out of them.

In the second place, Paul seems to be saying forget

*your successes and press onward to the tasks that lie
ahead.*

Of course everyone is proud of the glories that may
have been his, and it is right that we feel satisfaction
in a job well-done or an achievement that merits
praise, but "to gloat over a good past," says an old
teacher of mine, "may block the path to progress
almost as much as to grieve over a bad one."

It is good to have a heritage, a background, but it
becomes a stumbling block if we depend upon it to
see us through. Let us thank God for memories which
fill our minds with joys of days gone by, but let us
be grateful unto him for letting us forget our successes
as we turn to the tasks at hand.

Again, it is good to forget your guilt and past sins.
Let us go into this unguarded frontier this year freed
from a sense of guilt. To be sure, we must recognize
past sins and ask God's forgiveness, and, of course,
we never completely free ourselves from the marks
they have made upon us, but it is healthy to look to
the future.

Recall how Christ treated sin. Never did he con-
done it; never did he say it was good; never did he
overlook it. The sin of oppression and hypocrisy was
treated with harshness and consternation, but the
sin of frailty with tenderness.

He seems to say that we should think more of
what we can become than of what we have been.
After we have been duly repentant and have received
forgiveness, we must press onward, "Forgetting those

things which are behind." This is the way to newness of life. It is what George Buttrick had in mind when he said, "Constantly to deplore our failures and sins would leave us with weights upon our wings."

This leads us to the fourth consideration, "I press toward the mark for the prize of the high calling of God in Christ Jesus."

We are to forget what is behind so that we may reach for the new life in Christ, reach for the new chance that God through our Lord offers to all mankind, reach for the new beginnings open to everyone.

Paul uses the image of a race carried out in all its details. "In line with the goal I follow toward the prize." It was the custom to place the prize at the point where the race was to end. The vision of it spurred the competitors on to strain every nerve. It caused them to forget everything except the object— the prize. And Paul says he is looking solely toward the prize, which is not a material reward, but "God's heavenly calling in Christ Jesus," the prize reserved for those who had listened to the higher call of God.

What a wonderful provision God has made! Old things can pass away, and new things can be taken on. One of the most amazing facts of life is that all we have done in the past can be taken and fashioned in God's hands into a lovely mosaic. All the colors and broken parts can be fitted into a lovely pattern in the Master's hand. New life can be had in him.

AIDS TO WORSHIP

HYMNS: "O God, Our Help in Ages Past"
            "Lead On, O King Eternal"
SCRIPTURE: Phil. 3:7-14

A PRAYER

Almighty God, our father, who hast promised that where two or three are gathered together in thy name thou wilt be in the midst of them, help us we pray to feel thy presence in this place. Thou hast assured us that thou wilt have mercy on us and pardon our sins if only we come to thee in the spirit of humility. We come before thee asking that thou wouldst help us start over again. Though we come with broken purposes of good and idle endeavors against evil, help us to do better. Purge our hearts from evil thoughts and hard feelings toward those who differ with us, and grant us thy spirit of love which was in thy son, our Lord.

Comfort those in difficult places of decisions and give insight and wisdom to those in authority. Grant us boldness to face clouded situations and faith to trust all truth. Hear us, O God, as we lift our hearts to thee, for we need thy power and the healing of thy peace, through Jesus Christ, our Lord. AMEN.

19
Get the glare out of your eyes
(World Day of Prayer)

Margueritte Harmon Bro tells in one of her books about an old newspaper clipping in which someone writes about going to an artist's studio to see a new painting. He was first guided into a dark waiting room and left for ten minutes. Then the artist himself came in and explained saying, "I knew if you came into the studio with the glare of the street in your eyes you couldn't possibly get the color values."

The writer in the newspaper compares this incident with an experience had by John Oxenham in 1916 when he received a telegram from the British war department telling him that his only son had been killed in action. Overcome with so great a grief, he walked the streets of London until at last he came to the little church—All Hallows on Tower Hill. There he sat until peace came back to his heart, until the glare was out of his eyes. It was in this place at that time he penned these immortal lines.[2]

[2] Used by permission of Theo Oxenham.

Mid all the traffic of the ways—
    Turmoils without, within—
Make in my heart a quiet place,
    And come and dwell therein:
A little shrine of quietness,
    All sacred to Thyself,
Where Thou shalt all my soul possess,
    And I may find myself.

John Oxenham lived a very busy life. He was once a Manchester businessman, and, in addition, wrote sixty-seven books in thirty-five years. Yet, in spite of his busy life, he found time to go to some shrine of quietness many, many times before his hour of great grief.

In the fifteenth verse of the thirtieth chapter of Isaiah we find these words: "For thus saith the Lord God, the Holy One of Israel . . . , in quietness and in confidence shall be your strength." This message of Isaiah has a word for us today.

It tells us that we need to find a time and a place where we can pull apart from the noise and the glare of daily living. Unless we set a time during the day when we are alone, apart from the press of the crowd, the danger is such a time will be crowded out. Our lives are ordered on schedule. We go to work at a certain time. We eat at a fixed hour. We go to bed around the same time every night. We live by the clock. And unless in this crowded schedule we make definite room for prayer, we may find our day filled with activities that have encroached on time that belonged to God. We need to "take time to be holy."

This time out for quietness and prayer in our high-pressured life may of necessity vary with each person. Many have found the early morning hours to be most fruitful. It is then that our minds are fresh; our day lies before us unlived; our bodies are rested.

Others have found the close of day to be an appropriate time to review the day past in the light of God's eyes, asking forgiveness for mistakes but giving thanksgiving for the privilege of living it. Then before going to sleep it is a good habit to repeat these positive affirmations: "Into thy hands, I commend my spirit"; "God is love," "In thee I rest."

Surely, a time for renewal helps to keep the glare out of our eyes. Paul Hovey calls our attention to a sign seen frequently near many front doors, "Make all deliveries at the rear." Well, he points out that it is because of these deliveries at the rear that we are able to maintain the house. "It is the period of private devotions, the time of prayer and meditation, that enables the Christian to face all phases of life victoriously. Let us be sure we keep our 'service entrance' ever ready to receive the blessings of God."

Not only then a time, but also a place of quietness. It is to be some place—perhaps, a chapel, a church, an attic, a secluded spot in a park—but a place where we can keep the glare out of eyes, a place of renewal. We read in our Bible where Jesus "In the morning, a great while before day, . . . rose and went out to a lonely place, and there he prayed." Well, "a lonely place" means any place which will not be interrupted, free from the crowd. Again Jesus said, "But thou, when thou prayest, enter into thy closet, and when thou hast shut thy door, pray to thy Father which is in secret." He is telling us to get alone, away from "prying and approving eyes" to a place we make a sanctuary.

Anatole France tells the story of a young French writer who suddenly became famous. All Paris paid homage to him, and thinking that the experience might spoil him, France said, "You keep your head, young man," to which the youth responded: "Before I knew the drawing rooms of Paris, I dwelt in the Louvre and the great cathedrals."

There were his places of inspiration where the glare and glitter of the streets had been erased from his eyes and where he had seen life in clearer perspective. Look for some places today!

Ours may be a small room; it may be a tiny place; it may be a church or a chapel; it may be an open space. But it can be a place of quietness and a place for renewal where we can get the glare out of our eyes. "Thus saith the Lord God, the Holy One of Israel; in quietness and in confidence shall be your strength."

AIDS TO WORSHIP

HYMNS: "Love Divine, All Loves Excelling"
            "Be Still, My Soul"

Scripture: Isa. 30:15-18

A PRAYER

Eternal God, creator of all life, ruler of all nature, source of all strength, we praise thee, we glorify thee, we thank thee for thy great love toward us and all men. Into thy holy presence we come this day lifting our common supplications unto thee. Thou knowest the needs of our hearts; thou dost understand our fears and our unanswered perplexities. Meet us here this day, we pray.

But we would not only pray for ourselves and our need, but for others whose needs may be even greater than ours. For those brokenhearted through bereavement; disillusioned through disappointment; oppressed through hardship; burdened through a sense of guilt—be especially near to all these we pray. Grant as thou dost brighten the world with sunshine that some beam of thy grace and hope will shine upon their disappointment and bring gladness and gratitude to their hearts. In Jesus' name, we pray. AMEN.

20

When giving becomes a joy
(Stewardship Sunday)

There are many reasons why we should give money our concern in our Christian faith. For one thing ours is a money culture. Men will work themselves to an untimely death because of it. Nations will fight wars over what it will do. Politicians will use it as a means of controlling votes.

Again, Christianity is concerned with our getting and spending of money. Jesus refers to it over and over again. He warned against the dangers of money. "It is easier," he said, "for a camel to go through the eye of a needle, than for a rich man to enter into the kingdom of God." And yet he never spoke of money as an evil within itself, or as useless. He said that the test was what men do with it, and what it does to them. His use of rich men can refer to men of large or small means.

In his Parable of the Talents Jesus does not express disapproval of wealth, as such, but the use to which wealth is put. He says it depends upon the proper management. In his Parable of Dives and Lazarus, Dives is not condemned because he is rich, but because of the way in which his wealth is spent. He made it serve his own selfish ends and was oblivious to the needs of others.

But when men regard their wealth, great or small, not as private property to be used only for their own selfish purposes but as a sacred trust from God, then he said, "Well done, thou good and faithful servant."

Jesus saw that nothing determined character so much as the way we make and use money. We often say, "Money talks!" Indeed, it does, for if you get to know two things about an individual you will have a real clue to his character—how he makes and how he spends his money. Nothing throws a searchlight onto a man's soul as does this test.

So, let us turn to the words found in Luke 12:34, where Jesus utters a very searching and penetrating truth: "Where your treasure is, there will your heart be also." Surely he would have us ask some questions about our treasure. Where is my treasure? What do I care for most? What gains my first allegiance? What do I consider of supreme importance?

Jesus is saying here that our hearts lie where our desire or treasure lies. In other words, our interests in life soon capture our hearts. We become like that after which we seek. It was Marcus Aurelius who put it this way: "Every man is worth just as much as the things are worth about which he is concerned."

Then in the third place we should consider money

in our faith, for it costs to operate a church. And it costs to belong to the church, and it always will.

It cost in the days of old. It cost the widow her mite. For the sake of the church, Stephen was stoned to death. That it might spread and grow, Paul gave all that he had, finally his life. Judson went to Burma, Grenfell to Labrador, and Schweitzer to Africa, all for the sake of the church.

And the church continues to cost today. We could recount incident after incident of heroic service to the church in far-off places which cost, and cost dearly, many stalwart Christians.

This leads to this fact that when we care deeply, we give joyously. When we give joyously, it comes out of a heart of love. We give spontaneously. It does not have to be prompted. It is not done out of duty, but out of deep feeling.

You remember the beautiful story in the gospels of the woman who broke the alabaster box over the feet of Jesus while he was living. It was done impulsively. It was out of the overflow of deep feeling and appreciation.

When Mary broke that box and poured it over the head and feet of the Saviour, it was not a calculated act. It was not done because it was the right thing to do nor that it was her duty to do it. But rather it was done with a gay, reckless abandonment. She did not have to spur herself onward or tell herself that she would gain merit in the eyes of the Master if she did it. No, it came out of a heart that felt deeply, out of a soul that was filled with devotion.

This is the kind of giving that Jesus commends. Giving that is joyous and glad. Giving that is freely done. It is the kind that brings joy to the giver. It is the kind that gives not because it has to, or is expected to, but is glad to.

And we give gladly and joyously because we know that whatever the church costs it is reasonable at any price. This is so because it keeps alive our most cherished ideals. Jesus, from the beginning of his ministry, preached the sovereignty of the individual, the true significance of human personality. He told men that they were sons of God and important in God's sight. He told men that they should respect one another as children of God. And it is because our church keeps alive our most cherished ideals and principles that we gain joy in giving to the church.

Again, we give joyously because our church stands as a beacon for the weary traveler. It is a place of rest and a source of strength. It is here that men find God. It is here that they find a reason for living. It is here that life becomes worthwhile.

In the open doors of the church we seem to hear the echoes of the words of our Lord when he said: "Come unto me all ye that labour and are heavy laden, and I will give you rest." No person through the long journey of life escapes the craving for rest and peace. Busy as men and women are today, active in pressing forward toward some goal, ambitious as they are for honor or wealth, there comes a time when they long for rest and peace.

Wearied from the day's labor, worried from the cares of home, anxious about those we love, men need a place of quietness and rest. They need a sure retreat from the ways of the world, where they can be still and know that there is a God. The church, both large and small, becomes a house by the side of the road, giving comfort to the heartsick and afflicted, lifting the fallen, and protecting the defenseless.

So, "Where your treasure is, there will your heart be also." Jesus knew that those whose heart is in it give generously, gladly, and joyously.

AIDS TO WORSHIP

HYMNS: "Lord, Speak to Me"
           "Awake, Awake to Love and Work"
SCRIPTURE: Matt. 6:19-34

A PRAYER

Eternal God, in whom we live and move and have our being, in thee do we find our way in life and through thee our strength for life. Help us, we pray:

To be diligent in use of time;
To be faithful to every trust;
To be extravagant in thy service;
To be watchful of words we utter;
To be generous in our criticism of others;
To be courageous in time of testing;

107

To be aware of the needs of men;
To be slow to expose;
To be quick to believe the best;
To be responsive to thy voice; and
To be accompanied by thy presence;
Through Jesus Christ, our Lord. AMEN.

21

That Jesus Christ is Lord

(Lent)

      To say that we are living in turbulent times is but to play an old record whose needle has become scratchy. Nevertheless, it is true. We do not know what the future holds. Conflicting and threatening voices can be heard on every side; loud voices lay claim to our allegiance; and urgent voices demand attention. But it is the still small voice which must be heard above the din of voices today. It is the voice of God through Christ that must be tuned in if we are to be saved.

Paul spoke of this answer not only to his time but also to ours when he wrote in Philippians these majestic words: "Therefore God has highly exalted him and bestowed on him the name which is above every name, that at the name of Jesus every knee should bow . . . and every tongue confess that Jesus Christ is Lord, to the glory of God the Father" (R.S.V.).

What does this mean to us today? *In the first place,*

it tells us that Jesus Christ is Lord. Paul is here saying that at the heart of life is a loving God, whose suffering love for all men was expressed through Jesus Christ, our Lord, and that before such love men can do no other than bow the knee and confess that he is Lord, to the glory of God the Father. It is a name above every name, a new name which by way of his humiliation has won his place as universal Lord.

In calling him "Lord" he was asking the converts to the Christian faith to acknowledge that he was supreme, and saying that even a day would come when all God's creation would join in with the church on earth submitting to this Lord, to the glory of God the Father. Christ had been so utterly obedient to God that "the lordship to which he had attained was that of God himself."

It is this love that will win the world. It is this love which is at the heart of life. It is this love from which we cannot escape and which will not let us go.

Paul Tillich in his book *Shaking of the Foundation* puts it like this:

Even the greatest in power and wisdom could not more fully reveal the Heart of God and the heart of man than the Crucified has done already. Those things have been revealed once for all. "It is finished." In the face of the Crucified all the "more" and all the "less", all progress and all approximation, are meaningless. Therefore, we can say of Him alone: He is the new reality; He is the end.

110

Thus, the lordship of Christ is at the head of the church. It is to him we turn for guidance. It is from him we gain power to do and to be what God wants us to become. His mind is what we seek to know, and his mind is what we seek to follow. His way must become our way, and his love must overtake our feeble love. Forever we must hold him up to shame us for our littleness, and yet to lift us out of our sordidness. In his presence we are humbled and yet exalted. Bowing our knees to him and confessing that he is Lord is but to try to make our church more like him.

In the second place, it tells us that in the presence of such suffering love we are moved to love our fellow men. In the presence of such suffering love we cannot hate. In the warmth of this love we cannot mete out vengeance and wrath to other men. In the glow of such love we confess that he is Lord and all men are his children, that all men belong to the family of God. Someone has well said that we are never any closer to God than we are to those people we care for least.

Over and over again Jesus pointed this up to us. He said: "You shall love the Lord your God with all your heart, and with all your soul, and with all your mind. This is the great and first commandment. And a second is like it, You shall love your neighbor as yourself" (R.S.V.).

In the fourteenth and fifteenth verses of the sec-

111

ond chapter of Philippians Paul said: "Do all things without grumbling or questioning, that you may be blameless and innocent, children of God without blemish in the midst of a crooked and perverse generation, among whom you shine as lights in the world, holding fast the word of life."

He is saying to these Philippians that "living in a corrupt heathen society they are to stand out as God's children, showing by their lives to the people around them that they belong to God." Listen again to his fine image, "among whom you shine as lights in the world."

It suggests to us that as Christians we should be "lightgivers" to the world around us, that we should carry lanterns by which others might be guided. Christians then are "children of God, and the light they diffuse is from a heavenly source, like that of the stars. Looking on them men become conscious of a higher world, since in this one they are living in the spirit of Christ." [3]

And it is in his light that we find our hope in the darkness of this world. We do not know what is ahead; we do not know what decisions we will have to make; we are persuaded that he is able to keep that which we have committed unto him until that day.

[3] *The Interpreter's Bible* (Nashville: Abingdon Press, 1955) vol. 11, p. 66.

AIDS TO WORSHIP

HYMNS: "All Hail the Power of Jesus' Name"
          "Fairest Lord Jesus"
SCRIPTURE: Phil. 2:5-11

A PRAYER

O God, in whose love we learn the meaning and through whose strength we bear the burden and cross of life, give us the courage to stand for truth and righteousness even if it requires cost to ourselves. Grant that people may know what it means to sacrifice when they look at our lives, that they may understand the meaning of Jesus' command to return good for evil, to do good to those who hate you. Help us so to love that men might see some reflection of thy unending love for all men. Grant that by our lives we may bear witness to our faith that any man who trusts in Christ becomes a new creature. Give to us, we pray, the consciousness of thy Holy Spirit which guides us and empowers us and strengthens us. Send us forth to live at our best, through Jesus Christ our Lord. AMEN.

22

What Easter started
(Easter)

Let us look at what was started that first Easter morning. Of course, you cannot separate the events of that first Easter from all that led up to it—from the long years of preparation anticipating the coming of the Messiah, from his unique birth in a humble stable, from his matchless life, and his sacrificial death. All that leads up to that first Easter is in reality part of it and inseparable. Yet, had it not been for Easter and the fact and mystery of the Resurrection, we would have no Christian faith today. Let us look at the claim of Christianity which comes out of that first Easter.

In the first place the Christian faith claims that Jesus Christ is God manifested in the flesh. In him we find our clue to God. Paul put it like this: "God was in Christ, reconciling the world unto himself."

This all followed the resurrection. Of course the disciples were stunned at first by the news and the evidence of the resurrection. It was incredible as good news; but it became credible good news. It was too good not to be true.

114

But the fact and mystery of the resurrection does not rest primarily on the gospel accounts of it. Far more convincing, as someone puts it, "has been the historic fact of the Christian Church with its unceasing testimony to an indwelling Lord." It is a fact that quickened the Christian church and sustained it through the years. The impact of Christ's resurrection hurled missionaries 25,000 miles around the globe and has shaken the earth for nineteen centuries.

In our imagination we catch something of the joy brought the disciples that first Easter morn on hearing these words: "The Lord is risen!" After the crucifixion, they scattered in despair. They knew not which way to turn, for the light of their lives had gone out. Peter was brokenhearted over his denial, and the others weighted down for having run away. But on that morning new power came into their lives, for they knew their Lord had risen and was with them always. They became men of strength, joyous, and overflowing with life.

It was the resurrection that made men know that God was in Christ. He is God's revelation in a person. As Nels F. S. Ferré puts it: "Christ is God's communication to the world." Christ is God's love for the world. He is God as love becomes flesh. Christ is the love of God come to full fruition in man.

What a wonderful way in which God chose to make himself fully known—to come down to earth and walk among men—to become man! It is almost too good to be true, and yet too good not to be true. For in Christ we can understand God, that is all we need to know about him—that part which touches our lives. Now we know that the great God is personal in his being and in his concern.

In the second place the Christian faith claims not only that God lived in Jesus Christ in a human life many years ago, but is still alive in our midst today. This is the most important fact in life—that Christ is alive in our midst, that he is here doing for men what he did in the long ago when he walked physically in their midst—that is, changing lives, making new creatures out of old.

Leslie Weatherhead reminds us that when Jesus lived in the flesh among men it was not so much what he said that changed their lives, but rather it was the fact of his friendship. Simple men and women were changed; simple peasants and fishermen and housewives became saints. And the only explanation the world could offer to account for the change that had come over them is stated very simply in the New Testament: "They had been with Jesus."

So, if the claim is true that Christianity makes today—that Jesus is still alive, working, and moving among men—then indeed it does make for good news!

When we look back on that first Easter and the events which followed, the most convincing evidence of the resurrection is the new power in life and death which the world saw in changed men. There was something which transformed Simon into the rock-like Peter, and which changed the bigoted young Pharisee, Saul of Tarsus, into the Christlike Paul.

"It was not," as someone has said, "the memory of a Galilean carpenter, but the resurrection and the living Christ which made Jesus the chief regenerative power in the world's history."

Today this same spirit is here waiting to touch our lives and put new life into them. The risen Christ is one who turns our sorrows into abiding joy; our fear into courage; routine and dullness into thrilling adventure. He can take a person without a purpose or direction and give him a reason for living and a cause worth dying for. He takes us who do not want to live and makes us fall in love with life again. Thus, we have this good news which started with the fact of the resurrection that first Easter, "Lo, I am with you alway even unto the end of the world."

Some time ago a man related an experience he had during the last war. He was on a hill during a battle in the Pacific with seven of his comrades. After an attack he was the only one left and cut off from his company. There he was—one out of seven—and scared to death. Fear was with him.

He began to pray as he had never prayed before. It took him back in memory to the little country church where he had been brought up, his home, his family, his friends. He thought of pastors he had known and especially of the one who had meant so

117

much to him. He prayed as he had never prayed before. Then something happened. He felt a peace there in the midst of battle which he had never felt before. He could not explain it, but he knew that he had made contact with some power greater than himself which brought him this calm and peace. Now he cannot get away from that experience. It comes back to him over and over again. And now in the midst of trouble and trial his mind goes back to it and to the God who drew near to him.

It was the resurrected Christ reaching out to him. It was the Holy Spirit of God in Christ that made him calm and pervaded his being with peace. No one can convince him that this experience was not real, nor that the reality of the unseen world is not a fact. He knows something happened. He knows God reached out to him in an hour of great trial and in a time of aching fear.

So, he can change your life, lift you from darkness into light, from fear to faith, from death to life. Indeed, we do believe that he is risen, and that he is alive forevermore!

AIDS TO WORSHIP

HYMNS: "O for a Thousand Tongues to Sing"
           "Christ the Lord Is Risen Today"
SCRIPTURE: Matt. 28:1-8

A PRAYER

O thou eternal God, who remainest the same though all else fades, who changest not with our changing moods, who leavest us not when we leave thee, we open our minds and our hearts unto thee, this Easter day.

With gratitude we turn our thoughts toward thy mercy and love made known in so many ways. We know that thou art with us and blessing us even when we are unaware of thy presence. We are confident that thou dost will for our lives all that is good. We are assured through Christ, our Lord, that thou dost go with us in all life's experiences and that the very hairs of our head are numbered.

Be with all whose hearts have been made heavy through loss of loved ones. Bind up their wounds through the assurances of thy love and in thy unfailing promises. Lift our eyes beyond the shadows of earth and help us to see the light of eternity, through Jesus Christ, our Lord. AMEN.

23
"What doth the Lord require?"
(Christian Family Week)

Let us turn our thoughts to a little verse which has been called "the greatest saying of the Old Testament." It is found in Micah 6:8; "He hath shewed thee, O man, what is good; and what doth the Lord require of thee, but to do justly, and to love mercy, and to walk humbly with thy God?"

In the first place, it tells us that life is best lived under pressure. It is the pressure of life that brings out the best within us. The demands of life call forth the finest. What doth the Lord require of thee? This suggests that there are certain disciplines about life which make life good.

Even dogs have to be disciplined. In large cities people who own dogs must have them under control or else fastened to a leash. The seeing-eye dog is the college graduate of all dogs. It is a wonderful dog. It is not born that way. It has to be disciplined, to be trained. It has to value the life of its master even more than its own.

And human beings are their best when they live under discipline, under the pressure of certain standards and certain expectations. We have to subject ourselves to discipline. We are at our best, not when we are on vacation, and vacations have a wonderful part to play in the rhythm of life, but when we are on the job meeting life's daily demands.

Parents should expect a lot from their children. They should expect them to act in a certain way. It is the disciplined child that is the best child. Education brings with it certain expectation of discipline from her products. Society expects more of a college graduate. This expectation strengthens our restraints. Expecting the best from ourselves, from each other —all this plays a part.

Religion itself is a restraint. It places upon us certain disciplines which are good for us. Micah, our prophet who spoke these words, was a rough peasant from an outlying village far from the feverish rush of crowded cities. He was a prophet who spoke in behalf of social justice and righteousness. Micah heard God's voice in the agonized cry of suffering and need that rose from the throats of his downtrodden neighbors and friends. His was not a time of the worship of heathen gods nor of laxness in religious observance. There were temples and altars and shrines in abundance, and sacrifices smoked on every altar. Tithes were paid with regularity. Religion was well patronized and supported. *But there was no heart in it.* The poor were oppressed, and the priests were so lacking in true religion that they robbed the worshipers. Faith was merely formal lip service. They lacked restraints. There was no discipline of the spirit. And no amount of formal religion could make up for moral laxity.

What does God require of us all? What sort of restraints does he place around us?

First, to do justly. When we think of justice, we think of righteousness, goodness, integrity, conforming to the spiritual law, and so on. We speak of a man as being just, which means fair.

Could we not call it honesty? The prophet then says to us to be honest. To be honest in little things as well as big things. To be honest with those we like and those we do not like. Not to take undue advantage of anyone. To be fair, be clean. We are to be honest not only with others but with our principles, the truth as we know it. We are to hold fast to our code even when those around us are not following it.

We are told that when Crito came to old Socrates' prison to try and get him to escape by the help of friends, Socrates reminded Crito that they had long agreed that no man should either do evil, or return evil for evil, or betray the right. Then Socrates said: "Are these principles to be altered because circumstances are altered?" And so Socrates died by the decree of Athens and refused to do the least evil in order to avoid the greatest.

Second, to love mercy. When we think of mercy,

we think of forbearance from inflicting harm. We think of compassion and pity, the disposition to forgive, the willingness to spare. What does it all mean? Just this, *be kind*. It is easier at times for us to do justly than it is to show mercy, to be good and kind.

A little girl knew this when she prayed in a prayer: "O God, help bad people to be good, and all good people to be nice." That is, be kind. It is the kindness that we extend others which is the mark of our Christian faith. Jesus, you remember, portrayed this for us in the final judgment. Who were to be sheep as over against the goats? It was not determined so much by what they believed, but rather by how kind they were. "Inasmuch as ye have done it unto one of the least of these. . . ."

Finally, to walk humbly with thy God. Here is the note of humility as over against pride. Pride is the root of all sin. C. S. Lewis declares: "Pride leads to every other vice; it is the complete anti-God state of mind. . . . Pride is spiritual cancer; it eats up the very possibility of love, or contentment, or even common sense."

So the injunction is to walk humbly—not just alone, but with thy God. Surely when we walk with God we can walk in no other way but humbly.

To walk with God is not as mystical as we might think. It is to make him our companion of the way, to know that he is with us and beside us. It is to find the living Lord, the Christ, and keep close to him.

AIDS TO WORSHIP

HYMNS: "Love Divine, All Loves Excelling"
          "Happy the Home when God Is There"
SCRIPTURE: Mic. 6:1-8

A PRAYER

Dear God, who art the Father of us all and who hast established the homes of our world, we lift our hearts unto thee in praise for mothers and fathers. May this day be a day of special gratitude for our parents and a time when we shall do honor to them.

As children, help us to be worthy of their love and faithful to their trust in us. Forbid that we should ever forget their kindness to us and their sacrifice for us. Grant that the lives we live may reflect praise upon their love and devotion to us.

And to all parents give them the true sense of their mission and place in life. Help them to be noble and true, pure and loving, reflecting thy mercy and goodness to us all.

In the name of Jesus Christ, our Lord, we pray. AMEN.

24

A mother in a time like this

(Mother's Day)

Today devoted children will go home
for "Mother's Day" to express in flowers and gifts
their gratitude and love. Sometimes we say "this is
a man's world," but we know better, for the destinies
of nations and the outcome of civilizations rest largely
in the hands of mothers.

As we think today of the mother in a time like
this, we could do no better than turn to a mother
of olden days who faced a world not unlike our
own. In the first and second chapters of Exodus, we
find the story of a baby boy and his devoted mother.
You recall how Pharaoh, the king of Egypt, charged
his people saying, "Every son that is born to the
Hebrews you shall cast into the Nile" (R.S.V.). This
proclamation brought with it fear and anguish for
all slave-mothers of this persecuted race, for the
yellow Nile promised to run red with the blood of
their slain babies.

But the mother of one promising baby determined

to save the life of her child. "When she saw that he was a goodly child, she hid him. . . . And when she could hide him no longer" she placed him in a waterproof basket of bulrushes upon the broad bosom of the Nile (R.S.V.).

When Pharaoh's daughter came to the river's edge to bathe, she saw the child in the ark of bulrushes. We read "Behold, the babe wept!" Then the womanly sympathies went out in concern for this child, and the Princess decided to adopt him as her own. And by the skillful promptings of the sister Miriam the babe was given under royal sanction into the care of its own mother until such time as he was able to live in the royal palace. Jochebed was given charge of her own child when the Princess, little suspecting the relationship said, "Take this child away, and nurse it for me, and I will give thee thy wages" (Exod. 2:9).

What a magnificent plot! There is no story in modern fiction which will surpass it. What must have transpired in that mother's mind when she realized the privilege that was hers! She knew she had charge for only a short time, and then he would be taken to a strange home among foreign people. With what tenderness and care she must have dressed him and prepared his meals. The time was too short to fail to make the best of every day in his training.

But what a difference those few months or short years meant in the life of Moses! What a job his mother did to plant within his little life truths that never died! From a humble Hebrew slave home he went to the Royal Palace to become the son of the Princess, but he never got away from his early training.

How much of his high quality of heart and mind was due to the care of the mother who bore him and who nursed him? Charles R. Brown has said that great men have sometimes had great fathers, but they have always had great mothers. Susannah Wesley and Nancy Hanks Lincoln are but representatives of an innumerable company of devoted mothers who have given to the world competent and noble personalities who have written worthy pages of history in the advance of the human race.

Although few people know the name of Moses' mother, yet by the fruitage of her son, we know a great deal about her character and what she did for her son. Let us look at what she did and what it tells us today.

In the first place this story reveals to us the importance of a mother's care in early years. We know that she had her son for only a short time, and in an amazing way planted seeds in his little life that bore rich fruit in the years to come. We are told today that the early years of a child's life are the most important in setting behavioral patterns and outlooks. To be sure, knowledge, self-control, scope of mind, and perspective may come with advancing years, but the ability to acquire them, the attitude toward them, and the acceptance of such growth are formed in the nursery and living room.

Jochebed must have instinctively known the importance of these early years. For when Moses left her home and became the Pharaoh's son, he dressed like an Egyptian prince, but the inner man held fast to those early years' training.

Again we see during those early years the power of a mother's love. Can we not in our imagination see her lavish genuine love upon her son? Nothing was too good for him. No sacrifice was too great to make.

There is no love in life which can equal the love of a mother for a child. It is a love which cannot be bought nor destroyed. It is freely bestowed upon her children. There are dramatic instances in which this love is willing to give its very life.

You recall how the ancient city of Pompeii was destroyed by a volcano? A number of years ago during one of the excavations, the skeleton of a little invalid child was found in the skeleton arms of its mother. From the ring on the mother's finger there is evidence that she was of a noble family. She had chances to escape as the others had. But it seems that she turned back to rescue her helpless son. And through the centuries this mother's arms have encompassed the child she died to save. In these two lava-covered skeletons we find a mute but tender token of the deathless quality of mother love that will sacrifice self for child. Indeed a mother's love is one that will never let us go.

AIDS TO WORSHIP

HYMNS: "O Happy Home, Where Thou Art Loved
the Dearest"
"Lord of Life and King of Glory"
SCRIPTURE: Exod. 2:1-10

A PRAYER

Eternal God, we lift up our hearts in adoration. Thou hast made us one in our desire for thy fellowship, so we wait for thee to bless us with the benediction of thy presence. We thank thee that through thy nature thou dost make thyself known to us, and we would be more sensitive to thy presence. We would recognize all objects of beauty as thy handiwork. Help us to know that wherever we scatter beauty and loveliness, we remind men of thee. Like a scented flower give to each of us a fragrance of spirit which will add joy to life and make for contentment.

We thank thee this day for our mothers, whose gentleness and kindness brought warmth to our lives. We praise thee for the beautiful memories which cling about her life and for her faith in us which has given us confidence in ourselves and in thee. Help us so to live that we may do honor to her name.

Cleanse our hearts and hands that we may ascend to thy holy hill. We join our hearts together in gratitude for the gift of Jesus Christ who has shown us the way to richer, fuller, happier lives. In his name, we pray. AMEN.

25

Appreciation makes for happiness
(Thanksgiving)

Sometimes we wonder if what we are doing is worthwhile, if we really are needed. Then all of a sudden some kind, thoughtful soul passes our way and gives us new faith. He thanks us for what we have done or what we are doing. He seems to feel that our last visit, the recent letter, the short talk, the stand we took—made a difference to him.

We go home at night and childish voices express their joy in having us home again. A wife depends on us; a husband finds encouragement in us; a brother or a sister loves us. When the day has been hard, when cares have pushed in upon us, when mistakes have faced us—how a kind word warms our hearts and makes us feel we are needed after all!

What power appreciation has!

In the first place, appreciation is the chief source of happiness. William Lyon Phelps puts it like this: "Appreciation begets gratitude and gratitude begets happiness." Appreciation does not take life for granted but is grateful for it. Ingratitude makes for misery and unhappiness. A woman once said to her physician, "Doctor, why am I seized with these restless longings for the glamorous and far-away?" The doctor replied, "My dear lady, they are the usual symptoms of too much comfort in the home and too much ingratitude in the heart."

The grateful person is the happy person. Mr. Addison wrote in the London *Spectator* on the ninth day of August, 1712, these lines:

There is not a more pleasing exercise of the mind than gratitude. It is accompanied with such an inward satisfaction, that the duty is sufficiently rewarded by the performance. It is not like the practice of many other virtues, difficult and painful, but attended with so much pleasure, that . . . a generous mind would indulge in it, for the natural gratification that accompanies it.

It is a delusion to believe that only those who have a lot in life are the most thankful or the happiest. Some of the most radiant people have little substance. They make us think of the little line: "If a man is happy, he is not poor."

A person's real wealth consists in the condition of his mind and heart which makes for happiness. That condition depends upon how thankful he is for what he has. There is no greater virtue than that of gratitude. It is the basis of real satisfaction in life and real happiness.

In the second place, appreciation is the magic word which sets tired and discouraged men upon their feet again. It has a way of awakening sleeping powers within and helping restore self-confidence. William Lyon Phelps, a great teacher of literature at Yale University, after a long and useful life, wrote:

As a professional teacher I have had abundant opportunity to observe the developing power of encouragement and the sterilizing effect of scorn. People endeavor to live up to praise and to justify it; whereas cynicism and indifference will often extinguish a faint spark of talent.

He tells of asking a student one day to remain after class and telling him that his written work was excellent, far superior to the average. He says that the student's face was flooded with surprise and joy, and that he confessed that in all his years in school and college this was the first time any teacher had given him a word of encouragement. Dr. Phelps says that his subsequent career more than proved his worth.

Most people are sensitive to praise and to blame. It is so easy for us to hurt somebody. Dr. Phelps says,

Intent upon our own purposes, we jostle and shove our way through the complexities of social intercourse, leaving wounds more acute than if we jammed an elbow into somebody's eye. No decent man would kick a cripple; but there are many who suffer more from ridicule and adverse criticism, yes, even from lack of consideration, than they would from a bodily injury. There are many unfortunate men and women who have no particularly sensitive spot, because every spot is sensitive.[4]

There is no greater need in the world today than kindness and thoughtfulness extended to one another. A kind word, a thoughtful deed, a genuine appreciation, a friendly handclasp, a token of encouragement —such lifts in unexpected places and from unexpected sources have often changed the course of many men's lives.

In the third place, appreciation is not only the chief source of happiness, nor the magic word which sets tired and discouraged men upon their feet again, but also the mood and attitude which draw men close to God. Jesus speaks of this in the incident of the ten lepers who were healed. One returns to give thanks for what had been done. "He fell on his face at Jesus' feet, giving him thanks. . . . Then said Jesus, 'Where are the nine?' " (R.S.V.)

In a real sense their ingratitude was a worse leprosy than the physical disease. It is really pride that separates us from God, and pride is at the root of all ingratitude, a vanity which feels that it does not get what it deserves.

Sooner or later the grateful person is one who goes beneath the surface to the source of all life. Beyond

[4] *Appreciation* (New York: E. P. Dutton & Co., Inc.).

our debt of gratitude, appreciation to others, and our inheritance, we turn to God with grateful hearts.

AIDS TO WORSHIP

HYMNS: "This Is My Father's World"
        "Saviour, Like a Shepherd Lead Us"
SCRIPTURE: Ps. 100

A PRAYER

Eternal God, Father of all mercies and God of all comfort, we lift our hearts and voices to thee this day in grateful praise.

We thank thee for the good earth yielding her fruit and grain for our sustenance. We thank thee for this our native land and our priceless treasures of freedom; for thy mercies bestowed upon this nation and for the ideals of equal opportunity for all. We are grateful for the American dream that protects the rights of the minority and gives the individual a place of importance in our land.

We are grateful this Thanksgiving season for all who have given us a vision of the Eternal which has lighted our path and strengthened our hearts. We thank thee for all those whose faith has strengthened our faith. Especially are we grateful for the wonder and majesty of thy nature as we know thee in Christ; for thy love which will not let us go and which cannot be altered by life's changing moods. We thank thee that thou art near us even when we are unaware of thy presence; and that thy purposes for us are always good.

Give us grace to show forth thy praise not only with our lips but in our lives, through Jesus Christ, our Lord. AMEN.

26

The magic of Christmas
(Christmas)

What a wonderful day Christmas is! On a day like this the world is better than it has been all year. It is because human hearts overflow with kindness. It is because love is expressed more fully than any other day. It is because old grudges are forgotten, and past mistakes are forgotten and forgiven. It is because people are really better than they normally are. It is because they are more nearly what they were intended to be on this day.

What a wonderful world we would have if this spirit persisted throughout the year, and love as expressed on this day were spread abroad every day! Old barriers of bitterness and enmity are lowered. The Maundlebaum gate is opened from Israel into Jordan so that pilgrims can visit once again the Holy Places in Bethlehem and in Jerusalem. Through this no-man's-land these visitors pass without fear. It is symbolic of what would happen in our world if men listened to the glad tidings of angels first spoken in that little land many centuries ago: "Fear not: for, behold, I bring you good tidings of great joy, which shall be to all people. For unto you is born this day in the city of David a Saviour, which is Christ the Lord."

What is the real meaning of this day? Why all this rush of activity getting ready for it? Sometimes we may weary of all that goes with it, but surely we would not leave it out of our calender of events. For deep down underneath all the rush and hurry of this season we catch glimpses of its real meaning. We see its essential nature.

For one thing, Christmas reminds us whose birthday it is. The magic in this remembrance restrains us because it is Jesus' birthday. We should never get away from the thought that the reason we celebrate is because Jesus was born this day almost two thousand years ago. The course of human history has changed because of that birthday.

In the second place, this magic word Christmas reminds us of a love that is willing to forgive us all that we have done wrong and a love that asks us to forgive others of their wrongs. This love came down at Christmas time and enjoins us to pray, "Forgive us our trespasses as we forgive those who trespass against us."

In the face of such forgiving love one cannot hate. We are reminded of that love at Christmas. The shadow of the cross is cast over the manger. You cannot remember his birth without calling to mind his death. And if God can forgive the sins of men who persecute him and turn their backs upon him, who are we, being such sinners, to refuse forgiveness to those who abuse us. This is the magic we find in Christmas. Enemies are tempted to forget their differences and estranged friends are brought together.

If you have hatred or ill will toward anyone today, let the spirit of Christ get into your heart and forgive. If you have planned to get even, to seek revenge, to give back in double measure what has been given to you, get this magic word into your heart. What a Christmas it will be for you if the love of God through Christ floods your soul and drives out hate and bitterness and cynicism! Make it right with that friend or that enemy, and your heart will make room for the Christ child.

Finally, the word Christmas is magic, for it reminds us of the beauty and purity of a child, which as nothing else calls forth the best that is within us. It rekindles the sparks of manhood.

The contrast between what we know ourselves to be and what we see when we look at a child is sometimes the most cruel torment. When all else fails to break through the hard crust of our indifference, oftentimes the simple straightforward love of a child can call us to finer living.

Here is a husband and wife ready to take their quarrels to a divorce court, unwilling to understand each other, wanting to go their own selfish ways. Then a little child is placed in their midst knowing nothing of their quarrels, wanting only to be loved, and their lives are redeemed by the beauty and help-lessness of the life that belongs to them.

Here is a man whose self-control and moral decency have gotten away from him. He is on the downward road, careless with his money, faithless to his wife, shiftless in his habits. Then he looks into the face of a child and sees mirrored there in all its beauty his own ugliness and shame. The sparks of manhood begin to glow, and he starts the upward climb again saved by the radiance of a child.

And maybe you and I this Christmas will look with clearer eyes into the manger and see there the Christ child in all his beauty and purity, and seeing him be reminded of our own sinful selves. Such discovery can lead to newness of life. This is the magic of Christmas.

Robert Luccock calls our attention to one of the great passages of English literature occurring in George Eliot's *Silas Marner*. The circumstances of life caused Silas Marner to become a thoroughly selfish man. Hoarding gold had become in his loneliness and humiliation his only pleasure. Then one winter night a lovely child found her way to his fireside. Looking into Eppie's beautiful eyes he beheld beauty and loveliness that he had never seen before. He was shaken out of his selfishness. The little child had captured his possessiveness and self-concern. George Eliot writes of the transformation in these words:

In the old days there were angels who came and took men by the hand and led them away from the city of destruction. We see no white-winged angels now. But yet men are led away from threatening destruction: a hand is put into theirs, which leads them forth gently toward a calm and bright land, so that they look no more backward; and the hand may be a little child's.

These words describe what happened at Bethlehem. The hand of a little child was placed in ours to lead us forth toward a brighter land. That hand leads us to forgive. May the prayer of Phillips Brooks become ours today:

> O holy Child of Bethlehem!
> Descend to us, we pray;
> Cast out our sin, and enter in,
> Be born in us today!

AIDS TO WORSHIP

HYMNS: "There's a Song in the Air"
           "O Little Town of Bethlehem"
SCRIPTURE: Matt. 2: 1-10

A PRAYER

O God, our Father, who didst send forth thy Son to be King of Kings and Prince of Peace, grant that this Christmas he may be born not only in our memories but anew in our hearts. Help us come to this festive season seeking him, as did the shepherds of old,

139

that we may go home a new way—new men, new creatures in Christ.

O Lord, we stand before thee as one from whom no secrets are hid.

May thy beauty transform our ugliness
May thy love drive out our hate
May thy goodness penetrate our evil
May thy mercy forgive our unworthiness
May thy hope calm our fears
May thy humility shame our arrogance
May thy joy invade our sorrow.

O God, do thou mend the threadbare garment of our spirits that the star which first pointed the way may be the light that shall lead us out of darkness, through Jesus Christ, our Lord. AMEN.

✶✶✶

INDEX

141